CRISIS TO CHRIST

THE HARDEST AND BEST YEAR OF MY LIFE

BY STEVE DEMME

This book is dedicated to my ever supportive, always faithful, loving wife and my patient, forgiving, teachable sons who learned along with me.

May it encourage those families whose hearts have been turned towards God and towards each other.

"Let the words of my mouth and the meditation of my heart be acceptable in your sight, O LORD, my rock and my redeemer." (Psalms 19:14)

BUILDINGFAITH
FAMILIES

CRISIS TO CHRIST

THE HARDEST AND BEST YEAR OF MY LIFE

INTRODUCTION TO CRISIS TO CHRIST

This book chronicles the hardest and best year of my life. I did not see this crisis coming, but am glad it came before it was too late. I experienced incredible pain, and I discovered my Heavenly Dad likes me just the way I am. Even though my path went through deep waters, God was with me every step of the way.

The more I comprehended the grace of God, the more I was equipped to confront my own baggage and pain. I discovered I cannot hide my toxic issues for eventually they will leak out and hurt those who are closest to me, primarily my wife and children.

My motivation in writing is to affirm others who are going through similar valleys and tribulations. These hard journeys are normal for the Christian. Every person of note in scripture endured at least one life changing crisis. God uses these difficult times to work deep in our hearts, reveal more of Himself, and transform us into the image of His Son.

When a man confronts and acknowledges his stuff, asks for help, and draws near to God, it is my earnest hope this man will be healed and spare his family additional pain. This is the good fruit I long to see. May God help us as men, to do the real work of confronting our own pain. As we do, our wives and children will flourish in a safe loving home, where they experience peace, and do not fear their husband and father.

Since this book was published, I have added a one hour talk on the same subject online. You may watch it here http://www.buildingfaithfamilies.org/crisistochrist/. Other material will be added to this same site in the future.

OVERVIEW BY CHAPTER

In **Chapter 1, The Perfect Storm**, all the essential components of a storm of severe magnitude begin converging. I had been asking God to help me in several key areas of my life, and the answer catches me off guard. Thus begins the hardest year of my life.

When the storm does hit, the result is not pretty. **Chapter 2, Pain**, focuses on my life enduring the tempest. I wish I could say I was a stedfast trooper, but I struggled mightily.

God begins to draw me out of the abyss, and my healing begins. The life I had known is beginning to be renewed and rebuilt. My eyes are opened to the breadth of grace in a new way in **Chapter 3, Meeting Jesus**.

I thought the rebuilding process would continually improve but I reach my nadir in **Chapter 4, A Plea for Help**. Thankfully, the body of Christ stepped up and bore my burden valiantly.

God is alive. God is on our team. He knows what we need and when we need it. When I was the most needy He showed Himself strong on my behalf. A huge source of encouragement was several experiences where God revealed truth to my heart. Several of these special times are chronicled in **Chapter 5, Illuminations**.

With the new understanding of God's love and care, I am able to endure more valleys, but instead of grimly bearing the pain, learn to process and reflect on the source of my discomfort which leads to more healing. **Chapter 6** documents my **Ups and Downs** through this meaningful time.

Chapter 7, Blessed are the Broken, is my new beatitude. Being humble, needy, fragile, and transparent is a good place to be. It is not always pleasant, but it is good because God dwells there.

I can not put into words how thankful I am since these experiences have drawn me closer to God. I not only found grace for healing; I began to learn more about the Triune God. **Knowing God and Serving God, Chapter 8**, relates new insights into the character and person of the Godhead.

If I were to point to one turning point in my journey which has transformed me and subsequently led to good fruit in my relationship with my wife and children, it would be when the Spirit of God helped me to **Embrace the Cross in Chapter 9**.

Paul's prayer in Ephesians 3 has a phrase which I love, **Rooted and Grounded in God's Love, Chapter 10**. This language explains so much about my quest to know and love God. Roots are continually growing and moving deeper. They are not static. Neither is my relationship with God.

Almost every morning, my son with Down Syndrome locates me and crawls into my lap or gives me a big hold (longer than a hug). I need to find my Dad each morning and reaffirm my identity as His adopted son. **Let God Love You** and **Let God Define You**, speaks to our daily need and desire in **Chapters 11 and 12.**

Chapter 13, Deeper Roots, Better Fruit, examines my journey of reflection. The more I comprehend the love of God, the better equipped I am to confront my own pain and wounds, which leads to healing at a heart level.

I trust God more than I ever have. Knowing He likes me and has my back gives me confidence to ask His Good Spirit to **Search Me O God in Chapter 14**. I have stuff from my past. I can either confront my baggage with God's help, or watch my own pain hurt those closest to me.

Having walked with me this far, be encouraged. I am learning to abide in the love of God in **Chapter 15**.

God knows our frame. He made us. May we be found **Living in Grace** which supplies strength for today and bright hope for tomorrow, in **Chapter 16**.

CHAPTER 1: THE PERFECT STORM

He Sees Me

One fateful April day, I sat slumped in my car looking up through the moonroof. All I could muster was a desperate plea: "O God, help."

That morning I had attended a family board meeting where big decisions were to be made. As the meeting progressed, I grew more and more uneasy. At one point I had to leave the room, and as I stood in front of a large vertical window, pain like I'd never experienced began to sweep over me. I leaned against the wall and shook. Deep sobs emerged from deep within me.

Two of my sons saw my agony and came to hold me, but I put up my arms to keep them away. I stood looking out the window trying to regain my equilibrium. I felt as though I had just lost my family, my business, and my ministry. I was alone, lost, and without a compass. My world as I knew it had just been shattered.

Finally I was able to gather myself and walk to my car. I sat, not knowing what to do, and prayed, "O God, help." As I sat gazing heavenward I sensed God looking at me, and this verse ran through my mind: "To this man will I look, he that is of a poor and contrite spirit and that trembles at my word" Isaiah 66:2.

God met me in the car. His presence and personalized attention were never more needed. For that afternoon in April was the beginning of both the hardest and best year of my life.

How did I get to this place of brokenness? Six weeks earlier I had spoken at a large conference on the family. I was the CEO of a successful business and thought I was doing well as a husband and father. Now here I was desperate and alone, with only God to turn to. What currents had converged at just this point in time to create the perfect storm which threatened to drown me and everything I held dear?

Family Business Transition

A year earlier I had decided to change my company from a one-man show to a family business. Since most of my family was already working for the company, it seemed like the right time. For two decades my favorite talk to give has been "The Family That Stays Together Stays Together." Having a family-owned business seemed to be a logical progression based on everything I believed and espoused. Three of our four sons were college graduates, recently married, and now we could pursue business and ministry together.

We began having discussions about moving from an entrepreneur model to a corporate model with members of our immediate family becoming board members and owners. To aid in this transition, we enlisted the help of a consultant who was the director of our local Center for Family Owned Business.

In the process of being interviewed individually and then as a group, we were forced to think about our values, our long-term goals, and our relationship with the company. This sounds so simple, but the process represented months of meetings and hours of discussion.

When we met as a family, Mike, our consultant, would chair the meetings, and we would discuss our thoughts and plans. Having him present as an objective and experienced facilitator was a huge asset. Not only was he knowledgeable about family business transitions, he also had training as a family counselor.

With his calm presence, my wife and particularly my sons were able to discuss what it was like to work with and for me. Sadly, I began to sense that while they loved me and respected me, I had blind spots as a business leader and father. I also learned it was very difficult for them to tell me their concerns since I took input personally and often reacted strongly to criticism. In other words, I had problems, and for the first time they had a safe platform from which to confront me.

I recall one meeting in particular when I learned how I had hurt Isaac, Ethan, and Joseph. I was so moved I could not speak, and I wrote on a piece of paper stating I would resign from the company and turn it over to them. They passed the paper back to me and said, "We don't want your business, we want you." When they said this I knew I had to deal with my own baggage and not walk away from the table.

I have been blessed with wonderfully forgiving and incredibly loving sons.

A Line in the Sand

When the business transition process began in 2011, I was continually asked what my vision was for the next three to five years. Where did I think we were headed? What were my goals and objectives for the company? In addition, several young professionals had begun working for us, and before they committed to being a part of our team for the long haul, they wanted to know our direction and vision.

It may be hard to believe, but I never had a specific business plan. I had principles which I embraced and applied, but I had no specific goals, and certainly no plan for the next three to five years.

Finally, in response to the pressure, I was able to articulate my foundational principles: continue to improve the product and customer service, keep the prices as low as possible, develop new products as the needs arise, make a profit, and don't borrow money. In other words, respond to opportunities, treat customers as I would want to be treated, and don't go into debt.

In addition to managing a business I invested a good deal of time speaking on family topics and had recently launched a new website called Building Faith Families. For over 15 years I divided my time between running our business MathUSee and ministering at conferences. I also sent out a monthly newsletter and had written a few books for families. I wanted to continue the business as well as speaking and encouraging families.

Defining my principles and explaining how I had operated for twenty years was not enough for folks who wanted something more specific and comprehensive. In March of 2012, I returned from a successful speaking engagement and felt like I had a specific vision for the company which would also open up more opportunities for ministry. I was excited for I finally had a concrete goal and I thought my sons would be happy to hear what I had to say. At the first opportunity I took my Isaac, Ethan, and several higher ups in the company out for lunch and shared it with them. I thought my vision would be greeted with excitement and relief. It wasn't.

Then I communicated to my wife what was in my mind and heart. After a day or two, Sandi sat me down and said something like this: "Steve, you are one of the most generous men I know, and you have a good heart, but you can never do enough to please God and you're killing our family." Those words entered my heart like a knife.

I did not react in anger, I simply shut down. I lived in the same house with Sandi, but emotionally I withdrew and became distant. I was wounded and didn't know what to do. Her evaluation was spot on: I could not do enough to please God. She was absolutely right and I knew it. But it still hurt. And it hurt even more knowing I was hurting her and my sons.

It seemed no matter what I did, I couldn't please my family. For many months they had sought a specific plan and vision to move forward, which I could not give them. Then when I did put something specific on the table, this was unacceptable. I felt alienated from those I loved the most. On top of this, I was hearing about personal issues and areas which needed to be addressed, which was causing me additional angst.

This was a lot of information to process, and I didn't know where to turn. Up until this point in my life, I did not believe in facing and confronting my own pain but simply tried to move on by keeping busy. When I asked once why I had not heard of these issues before, my wife gently reminded me that she had mentioned them to me in the past, but while I had made changes that lasted for a period of time, they were not lasting.

On this spring day, when I felt like I had lost everything that was dear to me, critical mass had finally been reached and we all knew our family could not continue until I made real, long-lasting changes. In addition to seeing my world crumble, I was frightened. I had never experienced such pain; and it scared me to think I must have serious issues to experience such a deep emotional reaction.

Relationship with God

Another component in this perfect storm was my relationship with God. Around this time, I had been sensing in my head God loved me, but I wasn't experiencing His love in my heart. An old proverb says, "The greatest journey a man will ever make is the eighteen inches from his head to his heart." I was aware of scriptures and truths which convinced me theologically of God's care for me, but there is a big difference between head knowledge and heart understanding.

I knew God loved me intellectually, but I wasn't convinced He loved me as much as He did when I first encountered Jesus, when I had responded to the good news that God loved me and offered me forgiveness and a new start, when salvation was all new and wonderful. Gradually over the years I had begun to reason maybe God didn't like me as much as He had before. Perhaps He was a little disappointed that I was not living up to my potential. Maybe the only reason He loved me was because that was His job and He had to love people. This wasn't so much a conscious thought as a sensing.

I began to ask God to help me to comprehend His love in a new way so I would believe in my heart what I knew in my head.

John

Our fourth son, John, has Down syndrome. He and I have a special relationship. We like to be together and enjoy each other's company. We used to watch an old black-and-white western TV drama called The Rifleman. On the show, Lucas is a single dad raising his son, Mark. When we began watching these episodes, I noticed they usually ended with the father and son processing the lessons they learned during their adventure and then reconnecting. It was always a tender moment. During the closing minutes of the episode, John would reach over, hold my hand, and say, "You Lucas, me Mark." We watched the show years ago, but he still brings it up when we meet someone. He will often say, "Pop Lucas, me Mark."

The first thing John does when he gets up in the morning is come and find Papa. He calls me Pop; he calls me Steve; he calls me anything he wants to call me. If I'm still in bed, he crawls in next to me and just snuggles. If I'm in my office or reading my Bible, he gets as near as possible and holds me. It is not a hug, but a hold and it continues for almost a minute. Then he will kiss my bald head. This happens almost every morning.

Now, I know my wife would say she loves me unconditionally and Isaac, Ethan, and Joseph would too. I have a stack of Father's Day and Birthday Cards I keep on my desk attesting to their love and affection. But in my mind I am convinced if I'm a better guy, read more books on relationships, and go to marriage seminars, I will be liked more. It's probably not true but it's how I perceive it.

But Johnny is not impressed by what I do, how good of a speaker I am, or whether I have accomplished anything. He simply loves me and I love him the same way. We love each other for who we are and not for what we can or can't do.

My eyes are watering as I write this. The love John and I share is the closest I have come to experiencing unconditional love. One day I finally articulated what had been going on in my heart and said, "Lord, I'd really like to know You love me like I love Johnny."

Deuteronomy 6

For over 30 years I have been convinced the family is the basic building block for society. After creating the world in six days, God created what we know as family. He took the man and the woman, made them one flesh, and told them to be fruitful and multiply. This was before Abraham, before Israel and the twelve tribes, before Moses and the law. God designed the family. He crafted it. Marriage and family are not a good idea; they are a God idea.

I have studied the concept of family, designed small group studies for husbands and fathers, written a book about how to have family worship in your home, and made it the top priority in my own home. I know all families are dysfunctional to some degree, but still I am persuaded if you want to transform a church or a town, don't create more programs; focus on helping families. Healthy families are the foundation for healthy churches, towns, counties, states, and countries.

As a youth minister, pastor, teacher, and summer camp director, I observed committed families had a greater impact on the positive spiritual development of the children than any programs designed to reach youth. Bottom line, you can't replace Mom and Dad.

I knew as a Christian husband and father, my primary calling is to love my wife as Christ loved the church and raise my children in the nurture and admonition of the Lord. When these discussions first began about having a family business, I assumed I was doing well as a husband and father. Even though I worked hard, my priorities were always intended to be God, family, work/ministry.

Several years ago somebody heard me speak on Deuteronomy 6:7, which I frequently quote at conferences. "You shall teach them diligently to your children, and shall talk of them when you sit in your house, and when you walk by the way, and when you lie down, and when you rise." After the session they asked me, "Why do people at these conferences always begin with the seventh verse? What about the two verses preceding it?" So I looked them up. "You shall love the LORD your God with all your heart and with all your soul and with all your might. And these words that I command you today shall be on your heart." (Deuteronomy 6:5-6)

It dawned on me that if I am to do an effective job teaching my children to love God, I must love God with all my heart, soul, and might. I cannot teach them to love His words until those words are on my heart. To be able to convey these truths diligently to my children, I must be applying them in my own life. How could I have missed this crucial truth?

I also knew it was possible for Christians to lose their first love, as in the case of the Ephesian church in Revelation 2:2-4: "'I know your works, your toil and your patient endurance, and how you cannot bear with those who are evil, but have tested those who call themselves apostles and are not, and found them to be false. I know you are enduring patiently and bearing up for my name's sake, and you have not grown weary. But I have this against you, that you have abandoned the love you had at first.'" I don't believe they had lost their salvation for they were still the church, but they had misplaced priorities.

With Deuteronomy 6 and Revelation 2 in mind, I began to ask God to renew my love for Him and to help me to love Him with all my heart. I knew God would answer this prayer because it is His will for His children to love God (see Matthew 22:37-38). When we pray according to His will He always hears us and answers."This is the confidence that we have toward him, that if we ask anything according to his will he hears us. And if we know that he hears us in whatever we ask, we know that we have the requests that we have asked of him." (1 John 5:14) God began to answer my request, but not in the way I expected.

All of these factors converged in 2012 and led to the perfect storm, my personal crisis: meeting to transition the business; learning of the pain I was causing in my family; not being able to do enough to please God; the lack I felt in my heart relationship with God; praying for God to help me to love Him with all of my heart, soul, and might; and asking God to help me believe He loved me as much as my son did.

Prayer

Father, believing it is your will for me to love you with all my heart and with all my soul and with all my might, work in my heart and help me by your good Spirit. Help me to believe in my heart, what I know in my mind, that you see me, know me, and love me, in the name of Jesus, Amen.

Note: In this revised edition, I have added questions to assist in processing the information in each chapter. Work through them for your own study, talk them out with your spouse, or study them in a small group setting, "for where two or three are gathered in my name, there am I among them." (Matthew 18:20) May God bless you on your journey.

QUESTIONS FOR REFLECTION

1. This book opens with Steve's story of a deeply painful experience. At the end of himself, he calls desperately, *"O God, help."* How did God meet him in that place? Have you had a similar experience? If so, write a brief version in your notebook. As you are able, share it with those reading this book with you; hearing each other's God stories is encouraging!

2. When did Steve realize he *"had to deal with [his] own baggage and not walk away from the table"*? What gift did his sons offer him? Is there anyone in your life to whom you can offer this gift?

3. Steve states, *"Up until this point in my life, I did not believe in facing and confronting my own pain but simply tried to move on by keeping busy."* Do you do this? How has it worked for you?

4. Steve discusses his relationship with God and how it has been influenced by the pure love he has experienced in relationship with his son John. Do you believe God loves you unconditionally? Explain.

5. Describe what Steve learned from reading Deuteronomy 6:5-6, after speaking on verse 7 for many years. Ask God for a revelation of his love to YOU. Pray that He will help you love Him with all your heart, soul, and strength. I know God will answer your requests for they are according to His will.

CHAPTER 2:
PAIN

Desperate and Dark

Dante's Divine Comedy begins with this sentence which resonates with me, "In the middle of our life's journey, I found myself in a dark wood." Or as Dickens writes in A Tale of Two Cities, "It was the best of times, it was the worst of times...it was the season of Light, it was the season of Darkness, it was the spring of hope, it was the winter of despair..."

Even though I was already questioning my decision to change the business model, over the next few months we persevered through the process of setting up a family-owned company with bylaws, a vision statement, and all the corporate trappings. We were progressing—until I was asked to sign over the company to the family. It would no longer be mine, but ours. When the pen was in my hand, I couldn't follow through on what I had said, even though I loved and believed in my family.

I couldn't let go of the business. Most people recognize when a person devotes the better part of twenty years to birthing a company, it becomes a part of them. My company was more than my baby, it was my identity. It represented who I was. My fingerprints were all over the company, from how I paid our suppliers to how I related to my sales representatives to how I developed the approach to teaching. MathUSee was me in the flesh.

When I was in a good place, rested, and feeling philanthropic I would agree to make the transition. But by the next meeting I would change my mind. This was part of the hell I was putting my family through. My behavior was shocking, even to myself. I was acting like a child. I would reason with myself, "Sure it's tough letting go of your business, but act like a man and be an adult. Others have lost their businesses." Even if I did lose the business and became estranged from my family, shouldn't I be able to find comfort knowing God is God and He would work this for our good? After all, He is sovereign, isn't he? Hadn't I sung the hymn "When all around my soul gives way He then is all my hope and stay. On Christ the solid rock I stand!"? Where was my faith?

Instead I was desperate, as if someone was dangling me over a cliff and I was scrambling to find some kind of footing. My own behavior—especially leaning on the wall in the outer office sobbing and shaking uncontrollably—shocked and frightened me and made me know I had deep issues which needed to be confronted. I knew I should enlist the help of a professional.

Hurting

After the fateful spring day which shook me to the core, I sought the help of a therapist to begin addressing my personal needs. This sounds noble, but in reality I had been opposed to the idea. Many of my friends had benefited from counselors, but

I had been adamant about not needing a shrink. I am ashamed to say I told my wife more than once I didn't need one.

I saw no benefit in examining my past. I did not want to look back and review hurts and failures. After all, wasn't the call of God to seek first the kingdom and move forward? I did not want to look inside. Deep down I was afraid of what I would have to go through. I did not relish the idea of unnecessary suffering. I didn't want to experience pain and saw no benefit in doing so.

Having been confronted with my own pain, coupled with seeing the effect of my emotional needs hurt my wife and children, made me more determined to locate the root cause and address it. I was willing to do whatever it took to make lasting changes.

Not My First Rodeo

My first real experience with suffering came when my brother Brian died in a car accident. I had been a committed Christian for two and a half years. When I first heard the good news at a Young Life ranch in Colorado as a teenager, I had heard when I asked Jesus to come into my heart, He would forgive my sins, be near to me, and give me eternal life. I also learned of new life, joy, and the peace that passes understanding. When I chose to follow God more fully at the end of my junior year in college, I held on to this original message. The Christian life promises peace, joy, and new life.

During the summer between my junior and senior years of college, I worked as a counselor for a Christian organization which ministered to juvenile delinquents. With three months under my belt following Christ, I returned to college full of zeal and a desire to learn all I could about God and His kingdom. I changed my second major from math to religion and after graduation was accepted as a student at Gordon-Conwell Theological Seminary. I soon met others who shared my passion for God and eventually, through some remarkable providences, became a boarder at the home of Elisabeth Elliot. I had already read *Through Gates of Splendor* and *Shadow of the Almighty* before we met and had tremendous respect for her. She had lost her young husband of three years, Jim Elliot, to a spear from an Auca Indian when she was only thirty. She later remarried, only to lose Dr. Addison Leitch to cancer after four years together.

One night while I was sleeping in the downstairs bedroom, she knocked on my door to tell me my father was on the phone. I learned he had just identified the body of Brian at the hospital. On the way to the airport a few hours later, she told me one sentence which permanently changed the way I understood the Christian life: "God does not exempt us from suffering but transforms us in it." If I had heard those words on the radio or read them on a plaque, they would not have had the same impact as they did coming from her. She had lived those words. They were not a mere platitude; they had been received in the furnace. I had her repeat the same sentence many times on the ride so I would retain the meaning. I clung to those words.

I had come to Christ to escape life's problems. She with one sentence made me see that God does not exempt us from hardship but goes through it with us, and transforms us in it. As a seminary student who was studying theology and other philosophies, I saw how Christianity was vitally different from all other religions. Our founder was crucified and died. He rose again by the power of the Holy Spirit. He did not seek to escape the cross but embraced it, and the world has never been the same.

I arrived home to distraught parents and a younger grieving brother. After making funeral preparations and notifying relatives and friends, I was to speak at Brian's memorial service a few evenings later. When the evening arrived, I was at the church waiting to address our friends, family, and church members. I was empty and had nothing inside. A good friend who sensed my need asked if there was somewhere we could go and pray. We found a room nearby and knelt to seek God. While we were on our knees, God drew near. He was present. I know there were hundreds of people praying for me at seminary and my church in Massachusetts, and at that moment I felt their support and received the answer to their prayers. For the first time in my life I experienced two conflicting emotions at the same time. I felt intense grief over losing my brother, but I also tasted joy from the presence of God.

I arose with hope in my heart, spoke to the congregation about how God meets us in the valleys of life, and then extended an invitation for any who would like to have their names written in heaven to stand. God met us during the service and gave us "the oil of gladness instead of mourning, the garment of praise instead of a faint spirit" (Isaiah 61:3).

Cast Your Burden

My second wake-up call came when I was 34, when our son John was born with Down Syndrome. Over the first ten months of his life he had multiple surgeries and health complications. A serious bout with a virus left him in an oxygen tent at four months, at which time the doctors detected a heart issue. This was followed by catheterizations at six and eight months, open heart surgery at eight months, and then intestinal surgery at ten months. He still battles reflux and digestive issues to this day.

Good ol' me, who couldn't say no to any opportunity for ministry and who was always "seeking first the kingdom," was already overextended and beginning to show signs of burnout when this blessed boy arrived in our home. Let me tell you what I was "doing" and all of the hats I was wearing the summer John was born, to help you see the pattern. I wore the hats of pastor, part-time high school math teacher, director of summer youth camps, lobbyist for education reform in Georgia, chairman of the board of a children's home in India, member of the board of home educators in Georgia, and speaker, as well as a husband, father of three sons, ages seven, five, and two and a half, whom my wife and I were teaching at home.

When John was born and his health issues began to emerge, I burned out. I had difficulty getting out of bed and, what was most surprising, talking to people. I like people, and always have, but now I dreaded hearing the phone ring. Not only did I see the parishioners on Sunday morning, I saw them in our living room on Wednesday as well, for church assembled in the parsonage, where we lived.

This was the first time I had emotionally and physically run out of gas. I tried cutting back on my responsibilities and began resigning from some of these organizations. Eventually, when I didn't bounce back, I handed in my resignation on all fronts. I, and my family, needed to find rest and healing. We responded to a call to teach at a Christian school out of state and moved eleven months after John was born.

Surprisingly the next year was even more difficult, as there were challenges in the school and church we attended. One day I was at the end of my rope and God directed me to Psalm 55:22: "Cast your burden upon the LORD and He will sustain you, He will never suffer the righteous to be moved." Inside I was trying to keep myself from falling apart, and not doing a very good job, and this scripture guaranteed if I poured out my heart and placed my burdens on Him, He would sustain me and not let me fall apart. I tearfully met God on my knees and placed my cares in His lap. When I arose I began to heal and experience hope and a new lease on life.

You would think these two wonderful experiences of God meeting me in dark times would prepare and equip me to face this latest challenge. But while I knew suffering and difficult experiences were normal for all Christians, this crisis went so much deeper and revealed faulty thinking and deep needs of which I was unaware. I wonder now why I did not go for grief counseling after losing my brother. Why didn't I join a support group for parents of a child with a disability? As I ponder these questions, I think perhaps it was because death and a different number of chromosomes were so final I had to accept them. There was nothing I could do to change them. I couldn't bring Brian back from the dead and I couldn't change the structural makeup of John's cells. Once the initial crisis was faced, I could resume life as I had before. But the crisis I faced in 2012 was different; I did not have the tools, skills, or framework to process what was happening within my own heart and mind.

Blind Spots

How do I enumerate the ways I had hurt my family so deeply over the years? I did not see many of them at the time for a few reasons. One is my wife had been taught that a submissive wife is a quiet wife. She rarely pointed out how my words or actions hurt her and the children unless the situation escalated. When she saw her boys being wounded, then Mama Bear would appear.

In 1998 she told me I had a problem with anger. My first thought was she was overstating the problem. But after several months I agreed with her. I confessed my need to my fellow ministerial brothers and elders and asked for prayer. I read a book, *The Other Side of Love* by Gary Chapman, which helped me to understand anger better. I went to a seminar on anger and listened to a message about the spirit of anger, but with little benefit. I finally knelt by my bed and earnestly sought God to change my heart. He did, and I was helped for some time.

Life is hard for the oldest children. Isaac and Ethan rarely confronted me on my personal issues because they knew I would take their input personally and react emotionally instead of respond thoughtfully. I am not easy to approach when I am not in a humble, teachable place. Learning more about the gospel and becoming more rooted and grounded in Christ has made a huge impact on the way I relate to criticism and correction, but more on this topic in the next few sections.

During the potentially explosive board meetings, I was guilty of being controlling by issuing ultimatums and threatening to walk out instead of calmly working toward a solution. I would agree to a course of action and then change my mind. I did not honor my commitments and treated my wife like a second-class citizen. I did not always treat each of my precious family members with dignity and respect. I could be genial and humorous but I could also be dark and sarcastic.

If I were consistently the same way at least they would know what to expect and learn how to deal with me, but this waffling between two sides wore my family out. In the words of one brave son, I would genuinely and quickly repent and be humble and soft, but then I would swing back to the dark Steve. Not knowing whether Dr. Jekyll or Mr. Hyde was present left everyone on edge.

This kind of behavior is so not like Jesus. He was meek, gentle, and kind. He did not quench a flickering candle or crush a bruised reed. In other words, He did not wound a person's spirit with His words or actions. I, on the other hand, reacted strongly and said inappropriate things, and even though I asked forgiveness for my words and actions, those words were damaging and left scars.

More Alone

Before we could begin addressing family needs and the business transition, the most important need was my wife's well-being. The strain of living with me when I was emotionally shut down was becoming unbearable and taking a toll on her mental and physical health. She was bearing the brunt of the turmoil at the board meetings, while being emotionally cut off by me and feeling the pain of the rest of the family.

She could not continue to be with me without being in danger of serious health ramifications. Panic attacks and high blood pressure were no longer being helped by medication. Someday perhaps she will write about her journey, but for now all you have is my perspective.

We had a joint meeting with her counselor and my therapist and decided it was time for us to create a structured separation. This is not easy for me to write nor admit. But it is the truth. To this day I have difficulty even saying the word 'separation' and think of this time as a medical leave of absence. Sandi found an apartment and moved out for a period of several months. She began to heal and regain what she had lost in the painful transition process. I was miserable. I knew Sandi needed space, but I began to flail.

My therapist suggested I use this time of being alone to reflect and deepen my relationship with God. While this was noble and well-meaning advice, I was unable to follow his advice. I was screaming with pain. I didn't know then what I know now, abandonment and rejection are my two weak areas and affect me deeply. I was desperate and was unable to go with the flow. I felt I had nowhere to turn.

I wanted to eliminate the pain by running away but I couldn't because I was committed, I had pledged my troth. I couldn't flee but had to go through. Quitting my marriage was not an option. What message would this be sending to my boys, my grandchildren , and how will I explain my leaving to my son with Downs Syndrome? What about my testimony as a believer in Jesus and my stand for the family?

Adrenaline is supposed to initiate our flight or fight instinct. I was unable to flee, and I couldn't fight. Who was the enemy? In addition to my own struggles, nothing I was doing was working to restore my marriage. I was not in control. I was helpless and hemmed in. And I was alone.

Flailing

Some days I was okay with the decisions which had been made. They were still hard days, but if I prayed, read the Word, and sang hymns and praise songs, I could make it through a day. Other days were really rough. I fluctuated all over the emotional map, sometimes from hour to hour. When I was in a bad place, there was no other word to describe my desperate, frantic, childlike activity than flailing. Everything in me screamed to keep this from happening. I couldn't believe she had actually moved out and I was alone.

We were married. What about our vows, our covenant before God, our visible testimony, our commitment to marriage and family? I wrote emails to Sandi, sent texts, left messages, bought flowers, all in a desperate attempt to keep us together. I made promises to her, quoted scripture, and issued ultimatums. in short, I tried every tactic I knew to keep the situation from continuing. I am ashamed to admit I acted like a petulant child. Some of you are probably shaking your head in disbelief. You ought to. By the way, I had agreed to not text or email her so she could heal. Another broken promise.

I just found a letter I wrote to Sandi. The reason I looked for it is because recently Sandi mentioned that this letter, more than any of my other missives, meant the most to her. It was more of a confession than a plea to be different or a promise to change. It was not an appeal to return but an acknowledgment of my own lack as a husband. It was an honest assessment of where I had failed in my responsibilities to her. It was spot on. What is amazing is that I could write such a letter one day and the next day act like a fool. But this gives you a picture not my tortured and conflicted heart.

Dear Sandi,

This spring, I finally saw what I wanted to do with my life. I was energized, focused, and had clarity. I had been asked by the members of our family over and over for 6 months, what did I want to do and where did I want the business to go. I had been giving a lot of thought to a life goal and a specific purpose.

When I came home and shared these thoughts with you, Isaac, and Ethan, I supposed this news would be met with joy, but instead the exact opposite result occurred as this information shook you and apparently our sons as well

Then in the following two board meetings I felt as if I was losing everything of value in my life, my wife, my sons, my business, my ministry, and thus myself.

I understand better than before how stressful it has been living with someone intimately who can never do enough, is always driving himself, and as a result his emotions are rapidly and without any warning, going up and down.

When you took courage and confronted me, I heard only rejection. I saw your action as if you were taking sides and I was on the outside. As a result I shut down towards you, as I perceived I had just lost my best friend and supporter.

Confession

In biblical terminology, I sinned by:

- Not treating you with respect
- Not honoring you as the weaker vessel
- Not nourishing you
- Not cherishing you
- Not serving you
- Not loving you as Christ loved the church
- Not living with you in an understanding way
- For wounding your spirit

In my own words, I am asking you to forgive me for shutting down emotionally when you were courageously pointing out my need and how harmful my behavior is, was, and has been to my own flesh, my bride and my wife who I pledged to love honor and cherish til death separates us.

Instead of embracing the one person who has stood with me through thick and thin for 33 years, I wounded you and treated you with contempt. In short I was a fool. I can only try and imagine how alone and wounded and vulnerable, this must have made you feel. I am apologizing today, and am willing to keep asking for your forgiveness in the future as the need arises.

As I look back, I know it was the right solution to have Sandi move out for a season, and knowing what I know now, I would do it again. If she had not had a good support team and remained true to what was the best course of action, I would not have made the deep changes I did. But I still did not like it, and it hurt terribly. I now see her as incredibly brave and courageous. I can be a formidable and intimidating presence. I can also be winsome and charming. But she held true through all of my clever strategies and manipulations, and I am a new man because of Sandi's, Isaac's, Ethan's, and Joseph's tough love.

Those painful few months cast me on God in a way I never had been before. I was forced to get help and make serious life choices, not half-hearted attempts to change for a season and then revert to my default settings. This structured separation, where we continued to meet with our counselors, individually and together, was the best thing for the long-term health of our marriage and family. Recently I looked Sandi in the eye and thanked her for her courage and for helping to make me a better man. We are in the best place we have ever been, but it took going through hell to get here.

I know now that she left because she did not feel safe, and she came home when she felt safe. I am often asked by wives in similar situations, for advice on what they should do. If you are in this plight, consider the resources produced by Leslie Vernick (www.leslievernick.com).

I am not alone in having my life change for the better by being married to a woman who had the courage to confront me. The first man I met whose life was changed because of input from his wife was Ken Nair, the author of *Discovering the Mind of a Woman*. The second man was Peter Scazzero whose book *Emotionally Healthy Spirituality* had a profound influence on my life. And the last was my friend Peter Greer who told his story in *The Spiritual Danger of Doing Good*. To each of these men I am indebted for their honesty and transparency in telling their story. I need to say that I have other friends whose husbands did not respond with humility and learn to deny themselves. These couples are now divorced. Sadly, the wife was seen as the villain and the husbands were free to remarry and function in the church.

Walking in the Light

My first thought when these events were unfolding was, "Shall I continue to speak to families during this time?" I went to my knees fully expecting to contact each conference coordinator where I was scheduled to speak and tell them my situation and ask them to find a replacement. But as I sought God, two messages were communicated to me: (1) If conferences only invited perfect speakers there would be no one talking; and (2) He made me know I was walking in the light. That spring and summer I had received more light, and I was responding fully to the new information and taking steps to follow what He was leading me to do. I was meeting with my therapist and making progress.

Prayer

Dear God, our Immanuel. Thank you for always being with us. Thank you for revealing our blind spots. Thank you for transforming us in the dark and difficult seasons of our life. And thank you for always being at our side and faithfully bearing our burden. We love and appreciate such a kind and present God.

QUESTIONS FOR REFLECTION

1. Steve shares, *"I saw no benefit in examining my past. I did not want to look back and review hurts and failures. After all, wasn't the call of God to seek first the kingdom and move forward? I did not want to look inside...I didn't want to experience pain and saw no benefit in doing so."* What can you learn from Steve's experience?

2. When Steve learned of his brother's death in a car accident, what sentence changed the way he understood the Christian life? Have you experienced any traumatic life events? How has God met you there?

3. Record the differences between Steve's behavior described in the "Blind Spots" section, and Jesus's behavior while he was on earth.

4. Re-read the letter Steve wrote to Sandi, the one she said meant the most to her during their time of separation. Why do you think she appreciated it? What are your thoughts and feelings as you read it?

5. What essential things did Steve's wife and three oldest sons do that contributed to Steve's transformation?

CHAPTER 3:
MEETING JESUS

Colorado

When I was 14 years old I was invited by Kevin, a friend from my Sunday school class, to spend a week at a ranch in Colorado. I knew nothing about the camp except it was a really good deal. His aunt and uncle had offered to pay for him to attend so Kevin could hear the gospel, and he could bring along a 'friend'. I was the friend. By the way, Kevin and I had been the two mischievous kids in our Sunday school for a decade.

So in the summer of 1968, I boarded a Greyhound bus and began a three-day journey from Pittsburgh, Pennsylvania, headed for Colorado. I'd never been west of the Mississippi River. I didn't know anyone on the bus except Kevin. As I began to meet the other kids, I noticed a different spirit about them. I also learned we were headed to a Christian camp run by an organization called Young Life.

Interestingly, no one asked me if I was a Christian, and if they had I would have said yes. They didn't ask me if I was a believer, for after years of attending Sunday school, I would have answered their query in the affirmative. At some point I was asked if I had met Jesus. The way this question was framed went to my heart, because I couldn't say I had. I knew about Jesus, but I had never had a personal encounter with Him and couldn't say I knew Him.

A significant factor in this life-changing week was the setting for the camp. A few hours south of Denver, the ranch was nestled in the Rocky Mountains. I never tired of gazing at the panorama of the mountains and surrounding area. They had a profound effect on me and made me aware of God in a way I had never experienced. When I laid eyes on the Rocky Mountains, something inside me expanded. They are so majestic and awesome they made me aware of how big God is.

During the meetings and in the small get-togethers in my cabin, I began learning about the different components of the good news. I could have my sins forgiven. This was very appealing since I always seemed to be in trouble. I had been suspended from school at age twelve, and it seemed like I was always apologizing to someone for breaking a window or throwing apples or rocks at their children. I learned God promised a new beginning. Later I learned more about sin and disobedience to God's law, but at this juncture I just wanted a clean slate and a fresh start.

I also heard I would be able to know Jesus personally and talk to Him as if He were sitting next to me. Even though I had many acquaintances, I didn't have a really close friend or bosom buddy. I was more of a loner, even though I didn't like being alone. When I heard this part of the good news, I knew I wanted a friend like Jesus. The Bible says He would never leave me or forsake me so I would never be alone again.

I was taught if I prayed and invited Him into my heart I would have eternal life and go to heaven. This was not very real to me at such a young age, but it still sounded good. What I liked better was having Jesus with me and my sins taken away meant I would also have a joy and a peace which was different and deeper than anything the world had to offer.

When I put all the pieces together I thought, "Wow! Which part of this message isn't good? Now I know why the gospel means the good news." But there was still a conflict in my soul. After some internal wrestling, I knew I wanted to respond to the gift Jesus was offering. The speakers said Jesus was standing at the door of my heart gently knocking and desiring to come in, but it was up to me to open the door and invite Him in. After a few days I made my way to a secluded part of the camp behind a little Swiss chalet on the side of a mountain. I asked Jesus to forgive my sins and come into my heart. He did, and I knew it. I can't explain how, but at that moment I knew that He was real and He had indeed come into my innermost being. This is when I encountered the living God.

While I was at the camp, I learned a song entitled "He's Everything to Me" by Ralph Carmichael. It was newly penned and not yet in any of the songbooks. But someone made copies on white mimeographed paper with purple letters. (My older readers will recall this kind of copy which used to smell so good when it was wet and had just came off the machine.)

In the stars His handiwork I see,
On the wind He speaks with majesty.
Though He ruleth over land and sea,
What is that to me?
I will celebrate Nativity,
For it has a place in history,
Sure, He came to set His people free,
What is that to me?
Till by faith I met Him face to face,
And I felt the wonder of His grace,

Then I knew that He was more than just a God who didn't care,

Who lived a way up there, and
Now He walks beside me day by day,
Ever watching o'er me lest I stray,
Helping me to find that narrow way,
He's everything to me.

The words in this song encapsulated my new experience with Jesus. I knew there was a God a way up there. I knew about Easter and Christmas, but then in 1968 on a mountain in Colorado, I met Him face to face and felt the wonder of His grace, and my life has never been the same.

A few months later I entered high school and after three years moved on to college. During those years I had some special times of sensing God's presence at Christian retreats and Young Life gatherings in people's homes. But I was not a committed follower of Jesus. I remember one meeting where the speaker talked about all the things we run after to find fulfillment. Some try to acquire money as a way to be happy. Others think if they can find the perfect spouse they will be content. And the list goes on: recognition, sports, cars, etc.

Here We Go

During my junior year in college I felt like I had all the world had to offer. I was very involved in the life of the school. I was president of the fraternity and vice president of student government, and held other offices as well. I had a beautiful girlfriend, ran my own business in the summers, and owned my own car. Life looked rosy on the outside. But in my innermost being I knew all this world had to offer did not and could not satisfy my deepest longings. God was not real to me at this time because I kept Him at arm's length. But I knew deep down only God could really breathe meaning into my life, for behind the mountain chalet in Colorado I had tasted the reality of God. I had met Jesus. I knew He was real. As good as my life looked on the surface, I was not satisfied and knew there was something, or someone, more.

After my junior year I applied to be a counselor at a camp in the Pocono Mountains working with troubled teens. In preparation for this job I read *The Cross and the Switchblade* by David Wilkerson. Partway through the book I stopped reading and prayed, "Okay, God, here we go." It was not a long prayer, but God knew what I meant. I wanted to follow Jesus fully and seek first His kingdom, not my own kingdom or the kingdom of this world. I believe this was the time when Jesus became not just my part-time savior and friend but my full-time Lord and master.

A Time of Renewal

The year 2012 was, a painful period of personal reconstruction. My life as I had known it for over thirty years had just unraveled. I had to go back to square one and examine what I know about the good news. When I first heard the gospel in Colorado, I had no question at all Jesus loved me and He wanted to have a relationship with me. I knew He was the loving father of the prodigal son standing there with arms wide open to receive me as I asked Him into my heart.

For some reason, over the years, a little distance had entered into our relationship. Maybe God was a little disappointed with me. Or perhaps I had not lived up to His expectations. God was not as real to me or as intimate with me as He was at the Young Life camp. I began thinking God loved me more when I did wonderful things for Him.

Even though I knew in my head God's love for me was based on grace, which is unconditional, somehow I thought He would love me more if I behaved better or did more for Him. This unbiblical thinking nullified grace, since my connection to God had now become conditional. Without being aware, my belief about our relationship had changed from unconditional love and acceptance to God loving me and being pleased with me based on how I acted. Instead of a relationship rooted in what Jesus did, I had come to believe it now depended on what Steve did.

In the summer of 2012 God began to answer all my requests I had been praying, asking Him to help me to believe His love, to bridge the gap from my head to my heart, and to love Him with all my being. But I was surprised by how He chose to answer. I didn't anticipate such pain, nor did I think I would have my eyes opened to the wonder of God's grace in such a wonderful way.

I did expect to wake up some morning with a new sensation in my breast and find myself loving God and His Word with a renewed passion and interest. Instead, He began revealing His love for me. I remonstrated God and reminded Him, "This is not what I have been asking for. I know You love me but I want to love You."

Then I began to comprehend more of how God operates."We love because He first loved us" (1 John 4:19). God always takes the initiative. He is the great first cause. In the beginning, God. When I asked for help loving Him, He responded by showing me how much He cared for me.

I first began to take in how much He loves me from a verse I came across in my regular Bible reading. Jesus was speaking to His disciples when

He said, "As the Father has loved me, so have I loved you" (John 15:9). What did He mean by this statement? I stopped to ponder this one verse, and while several insights have emerged since then, at this time I received one simple message: Jesus loves me as much as His Dad loves Him.

I have no question in my mind God the Father and Jesus the Son have an incredible relationship. They are tight. They are in perfect communion and always have been throughout eternity, except for a brief moment when Jesus was made sin for us. Knowing how much His Dad loves Him, Jesus looks at us and says, "As the Father has loved me, so have I loved you." Those inspired words penetrated my heart, and I began to comprehend how much Jesus loves me.

Spruce Lake

Another significant step in my journey was coming to understand the breadth and depth of the gospel. During the summer of 2012 John and I attended a Joni and Friends family retreat at Spruce Lake Retreat Center. We had been going to this camp for six years and always looked forward to attending. During morning devotions each day the camp pastor would talk about a subject which had something to do with suffering or hope since everyone at camp has a family member with some form of disability. This summer I was pleasantly surprised when the pastor announced he would be speaking on the gospel, and for the next three

mornings he expounded on one verse, 2 Corinthians
5:21: "For our sake you made him to be sin who
knew no sin so that in Him we might become the
righteousness of God."

The most important insight I received was not
only was forgiveness a gift from God but so was
righteousness. I knew when I asked Jesus to forgive
my sins, He did. But I had mistakenly believed this
gave me a clean slate and it was up to me, with His
help, to build and extend the kingdom of God. I had
heard of the robes of Christ which cover us so when
God sees us He sees Jesus, but I had never grasped
the personal application of this idea. In Christ, we
have become the righteousness of God. When I saw
this truth, I knew I didn't have to do anything to
please God; I was already pleasing to Him because
I was in Christ. He has done it all. I breathed a
deep sigh of relief in my spirit as I listened to the
pastor continue to unpack this scripture for us
each morning.

Condemnation

Over the years I had lost much of a sensing
of the nearness of God, and distance had entered
our relationship. I never articulated or stopped to
think what I did feel; I just kept my nose to the
grindstone and sought to always be working to seek
first and extend the kingdom. If you had asked me
if I believed God loved me, I would have responded
that I knew God loved the world, so He must love
me. But my unspoken conviction was He loved

me more if I did more for Him and I did feel, as
Sandi had described me, I could never do enough
to please God. By never thinking I was pleasing or
could do enough, I felt I did not measure up, and if
I let myself I could quickly be discouraged. I would
describe this condition as a form of condemnation,
which is different than conviction.

Conviction is from God and is a result of the
work of the Holy Spirit in my heart when I sin. While
unpleasant, it is infused with hope, because I know
when I confess my sin, He will forgive and restore
me. Conviction is both painful and encouraging.
John 16:7-8 says, "I tell you the truth: it is to your
advantage that I go away, for if I do not go away,
the Helper will not come to you. But if I go, I will
send him to you. And when he comes, he will
convict the world concerning sin and righteousness
and judgment."

Condemnation is from the pit of hell; it is the
work of the "accuser of the brethren" (Revelation
12:10) and leads to despair. When condemned, I am
tempted to forsake hope and give up. Condemnation
is debilitating and discouraging.

Scripture illustrates the difference between
conviction and condemnation in the lives of Peter
and Judas. Peter sinned by denying Jesus, was
convicted, and wept bitterly. Miraculously he was
forgiven, restored, and became a leader in the early
church. Judas betrayed Jesus, regretted his actions,
gave back the money, confessed his sin, gave in to
despair and hung himself.

Peter is an example of godly grief, or conviction. Judas describes someone who is living with worldly grief, or condemnation. 2 Corinthians 7:10 sums up both concepts concisely, "For godly grief produces a repentance that leads to salvation without regret, whereas worldly grief produces death.

I have long sought to live in the reality of this wonderful verse, Romans 8:1: "There is therefore now no condemnation for those who are in Christ Jesus." I have lived in a state of semi-condemnation by feeling like I couldn't do enough, or be enough, to please God. Understanding the scope of the life and death of Jesus, and the subsequent gifts of forgiveness and righteousness, has helped me overcome condemnation in a fresh and powerful way.

Shame

I learned so much while I was living in and enduring this valley experience in the summer and fall of 2012. I have just explored condemnation, which I think is the Achille's heel of earnest Christians. Those of us who are most concerned about living a life which is pleasing to God are the same ones who are the most susceptible to condemnation.

Shame is another weakness for devout believers and differs from guilt. Guilt seems to be the result of something we have done. It is an action outside of ourselves. Even though I sin, it is at arm's length and outside of me. Shame is not about what I do, but who I am. It is inside of me. Shame is an attack on my identity and is equally debilitating. Guilt says I did a bad thing; shame says I am a bad person.

The fearful component of shame is being seen, known, and exposed. I dread being fully naked and bare before others. I fully believe God loves my wife and children and many of my other brothers and sisters in Christ. But my struggle is to believe He also loves me. For I tell myself if He really knew me, He wouldn't love me.

Just verbalizing the problem makes me realize how silly and sad is this argument, yet it has crippled me and kept me from living and tasting an abundant life. For God knows me like no other, and loves me still. I need to remember Jesus was sent to die for me when I was in my worst shape. He knew my sins and my propensity for sin, and loved me still. "God shows his love for us in that while we were still sinners, Christ died for us." (Romans 5:8) Even when He was crucified, He did not change His mind, but loved us to the end, saying, "Father forgive them for they know not what they do."

Not By Works

I now recognize an incorrect understanding of the gospel contributed to this major crisis in my life, and a more complete comprehension of the good news led to my healing the same year. Perhaps you will be able to identify in some capacity with this part of my journey.

When I was reading The Cross and the Switchblade, I had put the book down and said to

God, "Here we go," I threw myself into the work of God. People who know me recognize I have only two speeds, run and sleep. The following words which have been attributed to John Wesley describe my life as a zealous believer—"Do all the good you can. By all the means you can. In all the ways you can. In all the places you can. At all the times you can. To all the people you can. As long as ever you can". This statement makes for a wonderful attitude, if and only if, I am being led by the Spirit and being faithful to the work God has given me.

But after almost 40 years of living this way, I sat in our home in the spring and heard my wife tell me I couldn't do enough to please God. I don't know if I was always this driven, but this was my life now. I did not understand the unconditional nature of the gospel. I did not know I was already pleasing to God in Christ. I now believe that in Christ I am not only forgiven, I am also righteous and well pleasing, for Jesus is well pleasing and I am in Him.

This tendency to begin with grace and then move to works is not an isolated event but can be endemic to Christians and is addressed by Paul when writing to the Galatian believers. "For freedom Christ has set us free; stand firm therefore, and do not submit again to a yoke of slavery. Look: I, Paul, say to you that if you accept circumcision, Christ will be of no advantage to you. I testify again to every man who accepts circumcision that he is obligated to keep the whole law. You are severed from Christ, you who would be justified by the law; you have fallen away from grace. For through the Spirit, by faith, we ourselves eagerly wait for the hope of righteousness. For in Christ Jesus neither circumcision nor uncircumcision counts for anything, but only faith working through love. You were running well. Who hindered you from obeying the truth? This persuasion is not from him who calls you" (Galatians 5:1–8).

I felt salvation was a gift of grace but sanctification was something for me to do. I mistakenly believed the more I did for God, or the better husband and father I became, the more God would love me and be pleased with me. Finally, my courageous wife sat down with me and confronted me on this when she told me I could not do enough to please God. I was wearing myself thin, not doing bad things but spending my energies on my wife, my family, church involvement, the business, and ministry. I was pouring in every direction and had very little energy left. When I did notice I was running out of gas, instead of resting, I would read missionary biographies which made inspired me to work harder and be more zealous. Our family paid the price of having a fragile husband and father who lived with condemnation for years, believing he did not measure up.

When we hear the gospel for the first time, we all start with "Just as I am, without one plea" but then subtly begin to move towards "Trust and obey, for there's no other way to be happy in Jesus" as if we have to do something to earn God's favor. Sincere, earnest, believing Christians need to continually be reminded that salvation is always a gift. It is received and never earned. God's eternal unconditional love is not based on our behavior but on His character. It is not what we do, but what Jesus has done.

The summer I heard more of the fullness and completeness of the good news. I measure up only because of what He did for me. I would like to say all was rosy from this point on, but it takes time and intentional study of the truth to undo decades of faulty thinking. Change happens in the heart, but lasting transformation and renewal take place in the mind. I am still devoting hours weekly to being set free from old, default, unhealthy patterns of thinking and learning to walk in the newness and freedom which the truth brings. Much of my study on the love of God is found in another book in this Building Faith Family Series, *Knowing God's Love*.

Prayer

O God, set us from from shame and condemnation. Revive our hearts and renew our minds. Transform us in the truth of your word and reveal your great heart of love and affection for each of us. In the name of Jesus, amen.

QUESTIONS FOR REFLECTION

1. On the bus ride to camp in Colorado, Steve was asked if "he had met Jesus." What would your reply to that question be?

2. What was your salvation encounter with God like? Was it a clear, thoughtful, specific experience such as Steve tells in this chapter or was it a gradual unfolding in which you can't pinpoint the specific time?

3. Do you ever think that God loves you better when you are doing wonderful things for him? Read and ponder I John 4:19 and John 15:9 and ask God to reveal his heart for you.

4. What does it mean to you that "In Christ, we have become the righteousness of God"? (2 Corinthians 5:21)

5. What did a more complete comprehension of the gospel do for Steve?

CHAPTER 4:
A PLEA FOR HELP

The Email

When John and I returned home from camp, the truths I had learned were filtering into my thinking. I had new hope. I was accepted in Christ. I didn't need to "do" anything. He had done it all. The Lion had done the lion's share of the lifting (pun intended). I would like to say this was a turning point and I came home a different man, but changing the way I think and believe is similar to turning the Titanic. Deep-rooted convictions and entrenched ways of thinking take time to be transformed. God was patiently rebuilding my understanding of the good news, which was essential to my own restoration, but I was still fragile.

As tough as it was on that fateful April morning when I felt like I had lost my family, business, and ministry in a half an hour, the following Sunday was even worse.

John and I went to church, as was our practice, and after an inspired service I was feeling pretty good. But a brief conversation with some friends going out the door sent me into an awful tailspin. It isn't important what they said, for they meant well, but I went into depression in a way I had never before experienced. Pain is one thing, but depression is debilitating. I tried to read scripture, listen to Christian music, and do what I would normally do when I was down, all to no avail. In desperation I sent an email to 32 believers I respected. On the subject line I wrote 'Need Help Please.'

Dear Brothers,

I am in a valley and have been for a few months. But lately I am feeling overwhelmed by the battle to just make it through a day without giving in to despair and depression.

I know that our marriage is in peril. For the sake of her own well-being Sandi has moved into an apartment. Even worse, if it weren't for the effect a long-term separation might have on John, I don't care whether we get back together or not.

Sandi assures me that she wants to rebuild our relationship but needs time to heal. When I am in a place of peace, I willingly support her decision. We are both meeting with counselors and have a meeting for the four of us scheduled for July 9.

But when I am not in a good place, like today, all I experience is rejection, while feeling hopeless and helpless. And the pain I experience in times like these overwhelms me at such deep places in my own heart, that I just simply weep and sob like I have never done, even as a child.

I have trouble articulating all that is happening in my heart. Only God knows what is transpiring, but I need help.

I recognize the filthy work of the evil one, and the warring thoughts that are swirling in my own mind, but am growing weary of the continuous battle and feeling overwhelmed. I need your support.

Please pray,
Your needy brother,
Steve

I didn't know what to expect when I sent out my plea for help, but I was a desperate man. I wondered if people would call and try to fix me or if they would be silent. Within a few hours of hitting the SEND button a part of me was wishing I had not been so transparent about my own needs. The following was a part of a journal entry the next morning:

"I have funny feelings and mixed emotions after telling people how needy I was and then this morning feeling like I have exposed myself and am the emperor with no clothes."

But within a few hours of the email being sent I began to receive phone calls, texts, and email messages. The response was so encouraging. Even though a few men recommended books and sermons, most of them came alongside and were simply there helping me bear my burden and praying for me. A few offered to fly to be with me and said they could be there right away. I had tried to fight this battle on my own, but I recognized I needed the support, protection, and encouragement of the body of Christ.

One man said, "I thought you were superman." He was surprised to learn I was a broken man struggling to get up in the morning. This is the image I had portrayed for years, the devoted husband and father with a successful business and ministry, who was involved in the life and leadership of his local church.

Another brother called me regularly to assure me he was praying for my wife and me. He said he could not shake the prompting of the Holy Spirit to pray for us, and it was the first thing he thought of when he awoke. He prayed earnestly for us for over six weeks. These were true friends indeed and I am a thankful and wealthy man to have such support and encouragement.

In the Kitchen

Perhaps what happened two days later was an answer to the prayers of my support team, or maybe God in His sovereignty knew this was the right time, but while Sunday was the nadir and low point of the summer, Tuesday morning was the beginning of my healing and recovery.

I was feeling better, had just finished a hearty breakfast, was listening to uplifting Christian music, and was reading a book for Christians exploring the biblical roots for the Twelve Step Approach. What followed was too intimate to share in detail, but I sensed Jesus was present in the kitchen with me. He communicated one sentence to my spirit which changed the way I viewed my relationship with Him. In that one brief phrase He made me know that He made me just the way I am, He designed me to do what I do, and He liked me just the way I am. I began to laugh out loud.

I had begun to feel so worthless I was wondering if I needed a personality transplant or should reinvent myself. But in those choice words, He affirmed my identity and personality, built me up, joked with me, and conveyed His pleasure in me. This was the first of several encounters I had with the Spirit of the living God during the summer. I still am amazed at how He could pack so much important information into one sentence, but He is God and He knows me, and He knew just what I needed to hear. After all, He is the One who created me, made me in His image, and formed me in my mother's womb.

A week later I sent the following email to the same 32 people, giving them an update:

Dear Comrades in Arms,

A week ago I sent out a plea for help. You each stepped up to the plate in a way that was and is wonderfully overwhelming. I have spoken to many of you and heard from several others via Facebook and email. Your love, compassion, and support when I am in such a vulnerable position have reached my heart in ways I have difficulty describing. Your prayers and faith have helped carry me to a good place.

I have had two life-changing experiences with the living God this week. Jesus has truly appeared to me as my friend. I will wait until we can speak face to face to share the intimate details.

As I was praying once, God showed me that while I do need Jesus, I also need His body here on earth. As the body of Christ, you have each been used of God to demonstrate His love to me. Thank you.

But we are not out of the woods. Tomorrow afternoon we meet from four to six p.m. with our counselors. I am trusting and leaning and believing for God's will to be done on earth as it is in heaven. Thank you for being there for me when I needed you. You are true friends indeed.

Steve

PS: If you are able I would like to continue talking with one or two of you each day. It is so helpful. I am alone much of the time and need contact with men of like precious faith. If you are willing, let me know and I will work out some arrangement for that to happen.

Prayer
Thank you for the body of believers who help us bear our burdens. And thank you for being "our refuge and strength, a very present help in trouble." (Psalm 46:1)

QUESTIONS FOR REFLECTION

1. Have you ever felt vulnerable like the emperor with no clothes? Explain.

2. Re-read Steve's email call for help to his brothers in Christ. What important points does he convey? What in his email especially resonates with you?

3. Do you have friends you can call on for support and help when you are depressed and needy?

4. Steve says, *"I had tried to fight this battle on my own, but I recognized I needed the support, protection, and encouragement of the body of Christ."* What connection do you see between Steve's transparent request for help and the two life-changing experiences he had with the living God the following week?

5. Christ intends for members of his body to offer and receive from each other. This bearing of one another's burdens is also one of the things Satan tries his hardest to thwart. Think, write, and talk about your experiences in this area.

CHAPTER 5:
ILLUMINATIONS

Over the course of the next year or so I had several of what I call "illuminations." These were special times when the living God revealed Himself or some aspect of truth to my heart in a way which was unlike anything I had known or experienced heretofore. I believe any dream, vision, or revelation which God brings to us should be examined and found to be consistent with the inspired Word of God. I have decided to call these precious times "illuminations" because each of these divine communications have illuminated scriptural truths to me. I share a few of them with you in the hope they will encourage you as much as they did me.

I also believe God knew I needed extra help and grace during this critical time and gave me this special dispensation to carry me through a rough patch. I also know I did a lot more asking for help when I was needy than I did when life was smoother sailing.

So whether He was sovereignly giving me insights, answering the prayers of my brothers and sisters in Christ, answering my own heart cries, or a combination thereof, He encouraged and sustained me. In Psalm 46:1 it is written, "God is our refuge and strength, a very present help in trouble." He was certainly a very present help when I was in trouble.

No Baggage

One morning in October I awoke feeling like God was a million miles away. My first thought was I should find one of the studies I had made about how God never leaves us nor forsakes us, or something similar. Or perhaps I should get some good music and worship God and read my Bible, but I didn't have the energy. Instead I said out loud, "Do You still love me as much today as You did yesterday?" I wasn't feeling very reverent or respectful and simply didn't feel like doing the work of seeking God.

God graciously answered my request. I saw Jesus standing on the clouds with blue sky all around and His arms spread wide. He was laughing while He said, "Of course I do, I don't have any baggage."

As soon as I saw this image, several scriptures flowed through my mind to confirm this vision was indeed from God.

- God is light. "God is light, and in him is no darkness at all" (1 John 1:5).
- God doesn't get sleepy, or grumpy, or have good days and bad days. "He who keeps Israel will neither slumber nor sleep" (Psalm 121:4).
- God is love, all the time. He is not loving, He is love. "God is love, and whoever abides in love abides in God, and God abides in him" (1 John 4:16).
- God never changes. He is. "For I the LORD do not change" (Malachi 3:6).

- "Jesus Christ is the same yesterday and today and forever" (Hebrews 13:8).

I have this treasure in an earthen vessel; in other words, I am an earthy cracked pot. I am susceptible to changes in weather, my emotions, how much sleep I've had, and even whether I've eaten a good breakfast. I am a fragile creature dependent on many variables. God, however, is always light, always loving; He never changes. He is the great unchangeable I AM. I appreciated the picture of God standing with the clouds at His feet because it reminded me of flying on a commercial airline. On the ground it can be cold, windy, gray, and raining, but when you get high enough, the jet breaks through the clouds and all is light. It is a completely different world. This is God's country and here all is light.

The expression "I don't have any baggage" is important, because God is the only one who doesn't have any personal issues. However, every human has scars and hurts from their past. Nobody likes to readily acknowledge their own stuff because it hurts, so they guard themselves, their woundedness, and their brokenness. I asked God once why I liked some people easily but others I had to work at being able to love. He made me know it is our own pain which hinders us from loving and connecting with others.

I'm understanding if we really knew and understood people and could see past their defenses and weren't afraid to acknowledge our own issues, we could love everybody. Even though we all share in being broken to some degree, hiding and protecting our own issues reacts with the baggage of others and keeps us from loving our neighbor as ourselves.

I think of this special experience frequently because part of my baggage is believing God likes me and is always smiling when I approach Him in prayer. I struggle with seeing God as the father of the prodigal son always standing in the street with arms spread wide seeking to embrace me when I draw near to Him. Even though this is the image scripture conveys to my mind, I have had trouble believing it applied to me.

But I'm beginning to get it, and these truths are sinking into my heart and becoming a part of me. Now when I lie in bed processing the day, or when I first awake, I think of my Dad standing there with His arms wide open, smiling, laughing, and happy to see me and hear what is on my heart. God is good, all the time, in every way, and He loves His children to pieces, all the time.

I Miss You Too

One summer weekend I was speaking at a family retreat. In the morning session I had been speaking about the separation the Father and the Son endured because Jesus was made sin on our behalf. Generally when I think of the effects of sin, my first thought is I am separated from God, and until I ask for and receive forgiveness, God and I are not on the same page. I don't enjoy being convicted or experiencing this distance in my relationship with my Dad in heaven. With these thoughts in mind I had another meaningful experience with God that afternoon.

I had misplaced my Bible and was trying to spend some time preparing for the next session. I had just left the chapel and was walking down a grassy slope when I sensed the Holy Spirit whispering these words to me, "I miss you too." He was telling me that when I sinned it was not only I who missed the presence and person of God, but He missed me as well. I stood in that field with tears filling my eyes. To think that God loves His children so much He misses the connection with them when they sin and are disobedient! This was the continuing message to my heart, God really likes me.

A Stone House

One wintry day I was driving through Chadds Ford on the way to the Philadelphia airport. On my left was a beautiful stone house made of gray granite which happened to be for sale. I would estimate it was built in the 1700s or 1800s and I thought it was gorgeous. I really like granite houses and when I saw this one it struck a deep chord in my heart. There are not many "things" I would like to have, but I had a strong desire to have this house or one like it.

I started scheming in my mind about how I could afford to purchase it. I reasoned since I was approaching retirement age maybe I could sell our current house and buy this one. I considered a home equity loan and almost turned around to get a better look at the house and write down the real estate information. All of these thoughts took just a few seconds, when it occurred to me to talk to God about this yearning.

God had continued to be near whenever I approached Him in prayer, so I asked Him, "Why do I like stone houses so much?" As soon as I verbalized this prayer, God communicated to me, "I'm building one for you. I know you better than you know yourself, and it is going to be awesome." The thought I received was God was the divine architect, and since He knew what I really wanted in a home, He was designing one to fit my unique specifications. He was building it, and even though I didn't fully know what I wanted in a house, He did.

He also made me know He was joyfully looking forward to showing it to me when I got to heaven. The following scriptures came to mind:

- "O LORD, you have searched me and known me! You know when I sit down and when I rise up; you discern my thoughts from afar. You search out my path and my lying down and are acquainted with all my ways. Even before a word is on my tongue, behold, O LORD, you know it altogether" (Psalm 139:1–4).
- "In my Father's house are many mansions; if it were not so, I would have told you; for I go to prepare a place for you. 3 And if I go and prepare a place for you, I come again, and will receive you unto myself; that where I am, there ye may be also." (John 14:2–3).

- "As it is written, 'What no eye has seen, nor ear heard, nor the heart of man imagined, what God has prepared for those who love him'" (1 Corinthians 2:9).

I have lost the desire for a stone house. I no longer dream about owning a granite structure in this lifetime because my Dad is making me one and I can't wait to see it. I still like stone structures and they catch my eye when I drive past them, but the strong desire is gone, replaced with the anticipation of seeing the one He is making for me.

I have had other special times with God and have begun journaling about them because I do not want to forget them. They are more than divine visitations. They are an illumination of scripture and a revealing of more of the nature and character of God. I recognize God speaks to each of us differently because we are each unique. When words and messages were conveyed to my spirit, most of the time I sensed God had a twinkle in His eye. I like it when I sense Him messing with me. I know this sounds somewhat irreverent but He created me and understands how to communicate with me, and the jokes we share only make me love Him all the more. We genuinely enjoy each other's company.

Great News, God Likes Me

The central message from God's heart to us is He loves us. He has always loved us. When we were in a dark and hopeless place, God the Father sent His Son Jesus to reacquaint us with this eternal message. When Jesus bore our sins on the cross, a way was made for us to have our sins removed and be close to God now and for eternity. We call this the good news.

God not only loves us, He genuinely likes us. He knows each of us intimately. He formed us in our mother's womb. The Holy Spirit spoke through David these incredible inspired and eternal words:

"O LORD, you have searched me and known me! You formed my inward parts; you knitted me together in my mother's womb. My frame was not hidden from you, when I was being made in secret, intricately woven in the depths of the earth. Your eyes saw my unformed substance; in your book were written, every one of them, the days that were formed for me, when as yet there was none of them. How precious to me are your thoughts, O God! How vast is the sum of them! If I would count them, they are more than the sand. I awake, and I am still with you" (Psalm 139:1, 13, 15–18).

I would like to restate that not understanding the completeness of the gospel contributed greatly to my crisis. Understanding grace and the good news more fully and being rooted and grounded in the knowledge that God knows me, loves me, and likes me has led to my restoration. This is God's message to the world, and it is becoming mine. The knowledge and comprehension of the good news has changed my life, and I believe it will change the world, one heart at a time.

Understanding I do not have to accomplish things to please God because I am already pleasing in Christ makes a huge difference in allowing me to rest and not be driven. Knowing I am liked for who I am by one who knows me intimately allows me to be real and be myself and not work so hard to project an image of a successful man. But I still have a past with all the hurts, wounds, failures, disappointments, unfulfilled dreams, and sadness we have all experienced. Until I was convinced of God's love for me, I was unable to face and reflect on the pain I carry. This is why this section on the good news precedes more discussion on pain.

Prayer

Father, thank you for knowing us thoroughly and loving us completely. Open our minds and our hearts to receive the good news in a fresh way. Pour the love of God into "our hearts through the Holy Spirit who has been given to us." (Romans 5:5)

QUESTIONS FOR REFLECTION

1. After reading about Steve's first illumination, which attributes of God's character stood out to you?

2. Although God doesn't "have any baggage," humans do. We have wounds from our past. Where are you in your journey of brokenness and healing? Can you remember hurtful words spoken or actions done to you?

3. Have you experienced healing and forgiveness in your brokenness? How might your pain be hindering you from loving and connecting with others?

4. Which illumination, "I Miss You Too" or "A Stone House," especially resonates with your spirit? Explain.

5. *Understanding I do not have to accomplish things to please God because I am already pleasing in Christ makes a huge difference in allowing me to rest and not be driven. Knowing I am liked for who I am by one who knows me intimately allows me to be real and be myself and not work so hard to project an image of a successful [person].* What do these sentences mean to you?

CHAPTER 6:
UPS AND DOWNS

Buffeted

I wish I could write a seamless document of how I hit rock bottom in April then God met me in the car and my ship was righted and all was smooth sailing thereafter. I would like to assure you all was rosy after Jesus met me in the kitchen, but while I did begin to make steady progress through the summer, I still had lots of ups and downs. Today, as I was preparing to write this chapter, I spent a few hours reading through my journal for June, July, and August of 2012. It was not always pretty. There were times when I sounded rational and fully on board with the program. I genuinely wanted to give Sandi time to heal. I was trying to process what I was learning from therapy, drawing near to God in a new way, and seeking to be in the Spirit.

But there were also ugly angry rants. My spiritual pendulum swung between acceptance and patience on one hand, and wanting to fight, leave, attack, and run away on the other. I did not respect my wife's personal boundaries which we agreed to with our counselors. Perhaps I should give some examples, but I hope you will forgive me for not doing so. They are too raw and painful for me to include here. Today was the first day I have had the courage to go back and read those troubling words I penned in my pain.

I am aware there are very few quick and easy transformations. Rome was not built in a day; neither is a life changed in an instant. I was hoping for a quick miraculous change but it took time, prayer, intentional study, therapy, and a lot of support and encouragement from my brothers and sisters in Christ. I have journal entries referring to many hours of phone calls with friends from around the country over several months' time. Here is one journal entry I wrote in June about Nik Wallenda, who had just crossed Niagara Falls.

"Heard Wallenda speak on the radio this morning. When he went across Niagara Falls, he said he looked down and saw the swirling water, a mist kept him from looking ahead, and the winds were hitting him from the sides. But he kept praying and focusing on God. That is such an accurate description of how I feel. I see the problems if I fall, but I can't see where I am going or how much longer the journey is, then unseen currents buffet me and I am not able to prepare to meet them."

In retrospect I have found the more I became rooted and grounded in God and His love, the more able I was to dig deeper and face my own pain and baggage. I could not have come to grips with my stuff without knowing God was at my side and liked me for who I am. One experience does not a lifetime make, and over the next several months I dug deeper into the Word of God and continued to confront my own demons.

Alone and Reflecting

I spent a good deal of time by myself throughout the summer and fall. It is easier to try to bury pain by keeping busy and surrounding oneself with activity. Being alone for much of this time left me depending on God in a new way. My devotions were not optional; I needed help day to day and hour to hour. I read scripture, meditated on the Word, sang hymns, listened to Christian music as a lifeline to my spirit. I was a broken, fragile, wounded, needy man. I would be fine for part of the day, and then someone would make a comment or I would read something on social media which triggered a new emotion and I would immediately dissolve in tears of despair.

My first big assignment was to figure out why I reacted so strongly the day in the office when I felt as though I lost everything in one hour. After study and reflection, I discovered I have a significant problem with abandonment. This sounds dramatic, but I can't think of a better word to describe my state, so it will have to suffice. But first a little background.

One of the big components to unraveling the origin of my own pain was a five-day group therapy program called Breakthrough for Relationships which I applied to attend as soon as possible. They usually are full but they had an opening over Memorial Day weekend and I was able to attend. Some of my Christian friends were not thrilled, but I was hungry to find root causes and do the work of discovering where my personal issues originated. Why was I having so much trouble with being alone? Why couldn't I let go of the business? Where had my feeling of being abandoned originated?

In the past few years my mother had shared with me some insights I did not recall about the first five years of my life. I was the firstborn of three sons. I was a surprise. Even though my folks wanted children, they were hoping to wait a little longer before starting a family. My dad was a traveling salesman and was only home on weekends during my early formative years. As a toddler, I watched my father walk out of the house once a week and return several days later. How hard it must have been for little Steve to lose his dad every week. No amount of explanation would have registered in this little guy's mind. To this day I have trouble being abandoned or left out. Perhaps now you can understand how difficult it was for me to lose my family, business, and ministry that painful day in the spring. And then how much it hurt coming home from an emotionally draining week of relationship therapy to an empty house.

Life Is Hard

The reality of pain and the lessons I learned from it, while not on the same level as the gospel, has been an eye opener to me. When I was in the throes of my personal crisis in 2012, I wanted the pain to cease, my wife to come home, and life to resume a semblance of normalcy. I wanted peace.

I don't like to suffer, even though I know we all will eventually in some form or another. If we are sinners, then we are guaranteed a hard life. "The way of transgressors is hard" (Proverbs 13:15 KJV).

If we have chosen to follow Jesus, we will still suffer, but with purpose, with hope, and with the presence of God. "I have said these things to you, that in me you may have peace. In the world you will have tribulation. But take heart; I have overcome the world" John 16:33. In Romans 8 we learn that all things work together for our good and at the end of the chapter, nothing, not even tribulation, can separate us from the love of God in Christ Jesus. So we will suffer, but we have the presence and promises of God to sustain us.

I am not going to address the broad topic of suffering in this book, but I am going to focus on personal pain, for it is all around us. It must be examined and addressed with God's help.

Family Pain

Here is another red-letter statement: Much of my distress in 2012 was seeing my own baggage, my internal wounds, was hurting the most important people in my life, my wife and sons. I think of my own secret hurts and scars from my past as toxic waste. When I am rested, content, and at peace, then this harmful material is safely contained in a lead container and hidden on the floor of my closet. But when I am not rested, working too hard, and stressed, the toxic matter leaks, and it damages those who are closest to me. If for no other reason than this, I am continually reflecting and examining my heart so I can minimize the hurt to those who are closest to me. I am not as concerned about being whole for my own sake, as in minimizing pain for my wife, children, and grandchildren.

There may be people who love their families as much as I love mine, but not more. As a father, I sought to spare my family pain. Now I was faced with the knowledge that I was the source of it. This awareness was almost too difficult to assimilate. I have long been convinced that fathers have the potential to build up their wives and children like no one else. Fathers also possess the ability to hurt them like no other. This is the two-edged sword of parenting.

I have learned my past shapes me and contributes to my value system more than I ever fully comprehended. I am not an independent being. I am a product of my parents, my extended family, my church, community, and so on. The past is always present, even when carefully concealed. Unless and until I acknowledge my pain and address my scars, I will wound the very people I am seeking to bless. It has been said hurt people, hurt people. I had been hurt and I was now hurting others.

I would like to reassert what I said earlier in the book, our family has gone through a hell of sorts but we are now in the best place we have ever been. Take courage: God is able to use our pain for our gain. He is a wonderful Redeemer. The converse of hurt people hurting people is forgiven people, forgive people, and loved people, love people. My exhorter nature wants to jump to the next chapter on being rooted and grounded in Christ, but I need to address the pain which was instrumental in rebuilding my foundation on Christ alone.

Crisis in Scripture

As I began to learn about pain, I asked God where this concept is illustrated and lived out in scripture. My thoughts were directed to Joseph. We have been given an overview of the family dynamics of his parents and grandparents in the book of Genesis. We walk through life with Abraham, read about the birth and marriage of quiet Isaac, and are there when he and Rebekah were blessed with twin sons.

Through the obedience and faith of Abraham a thousand generations have been blessed, including his own son, grandsons, and great-grandchildren. We also see harmful behaviors passed down along with the blessings. Isaac and Rebekah chose personal favorites among their sons: Isaac favored Esau; Rebekah liked Jacob the best. This favoritism did not breed harmony in the home, as eventually Rebekah helped Jacob deceive Isaac and steal the blessing meant for Esau. This deception lead to Esau threatening to kill Jacob, which drove him away. This is not the end of the story, as a harmful trend of parenting was set in motion through this favoritism.

When Jacob had children, he chose a favorite as well, Joseph. This led to Joseph being hated by his siblings, sold to slave traders, and cast into prison. We know God used this whole string of events as part of His plan for the people of Israel and Egypt, but look at the toll it took on Joseph. When his brothers, the same ones who betrayed him, came to him, he first tested them. Try to understand from Joseph's perspective what he was feeling when confronted with these men who had turned a deaf ear to his cries when he was in the pit. These big brothers who he had looked up to had betrayed him. It is pretty hard to overlook this kind of betrayal and rejection.

Later, after they had gone back and forth seeking food in Egypt, they were recounting that dark day when they had sold him into slavery, not knowing he understood their words. "Then they said to one another, 'In truth we are guilty concerning our brother, in that we saw the distress of his soul, when he begged us and we did not listen. That is why this distress has come upon us.' And Reuben answered them, 'Did I not tell you not to sin against the boy? But you did not listen. So now there comes a reckoning for his blood.' They did not know that Joseph understood them, for there was an interpreter between them. Then he turned away from them and wept. And he returned to them and spoke to them. And he took Simeon from them and bound him before their eyes." (Genesis 42:21-24)

I empathize with others who have been wounded more than I used to since I have drunk from a similar bitter cup the past several years. When I read about Joseph, I hurt with him. I feel his anguish as he listened to his brothers talk of the painful day when he was sold and abandoned by his own family. He experienced afresh the bitterness of this awful event and had to turn away and weep.

He wept again when reunited with Benjamin, and wept aloud when he revealed his true identity to his brothers. Joseph may have been the big cheese in Egypt, but he was still the younger brother, and he had grief which was triggered by the appearance of his family. Even knowing God was using this situation to help these two nations through a famine did not diminish the hurt. For the experience of being sold into slavery by those he trusted, was still a part of who he was.

It is no mystery to me when he had to test these brothers who had betrayed him once before. Joseph had been burned and suffered as a result of their behavior, and he needed to know if they were true men. We can fast forward to the end of the story when his father died, these same brothers came to him, lying and trying to deceive once again. Instead of punishing them as they deserved, Joseph was able to forgive them and break the cycle of pain in their family. He was able to extend grace to his brothers. I love Joseph.

There is so much grief in Genesis which is tied to family relationships. When we have friends who hurt us or cause us grief, we can walk away from them and get new friends. We have a degree of choice with whom we associate. But when dealing with members of our family, we cannot un-choose them or walk away from them. We have a history together. We are a part of each other. Because of this and other factors, we are forced to deal with our own stuff and learn how to relate to our relations.

David

David's life is probably the most transparent one in scripture. We are not only introduced to him as a youth, we know how he lived and how he died. We have his private journal at our fingertips. His private thoughts, prayers, and poems are recorded in the Psalms of David. He is mentioned in over one thousand passages of the Bible. David was a man after God's own heart. God loved him, blessed him, delivered him from a multitude of perils, and made him king. God also made promises to him which extended to his lineage for generations because of his obedience, including the promise the Messiah would come from his line.

David was also human and made mistakes. His sins impacted the relationships he had with his wives and especially his sons. The kingdom of David was established and blessed, but the home life of David was in shambles because of his sin. His first son by Bathsheba died, and his son Absalom tried to usurp the throne and slay his father. When Absalom died David's grief could not be assuaged. David's love for his son is unquestioned, but they did not have a healthy relationship.

Another difficult and life-changing experience which shaped David was when he sought to bring the ark into Jerusalem. Bringing the ark to the city was a good idea and needed to happen. David wisely consulted the leaders and the people, and all agreed it should take place. But when the oxen stumbled, his friend Uzzah reached out to steady the ark and was instantly killed. David was shaken to the core of his being. (You can read the full account in 1 Chronicles 13:1-12 and 15:2, 11-15.)

When I read this account of David, I see a man who thought he was doing the right thing, the right way, and then lost his friend. He didn't know how to process what happened and he was angry and afraid of God. We don't know the particulars of the soul searching which occurred as David wrestled with God, but I believe he gave himself to prayer and study of the Word of God. A few chapters later he says in the thirteenth verse of chapter 15 because they did not "seek God according to the rules (ordinances)" Uzzah died. Because they consulted one another but not God's Word they made a fatal mistake. The ark was supposed to be carried by Levites, not put on new carts. After an intensive study of the Word of God, David reinstated the Levites and Priests and instituted new ordinances about praise, worship, and the giving of thanks in Israel. (You can read the compete record in 1 Chronicles 15 and 16.)

This dramatic event impacted David deeply. As he studied the scriptures and sought God to understand why Uzzah had died, the Spirit not only helped get his eyes back on God's inspired word, but on God Himself. I can relate to David.

Jacob and Others

I also thought of Jacob, when he had just escaped his angry uncle Laban and was about to meet his brother Esau accompanied by 400 of his men. Esau had vowed to kill him many years earlier, and Jacob was "greatly afraid and distressed" and "alone." He wrestled through the night with the angel of God and emerged the next morning a changed man with a new name, Israel. (See Genesis 32.)

Then I thought of Moses fleeing Pharaoh and meeting God in the desert; Abraham offering up Isaac; Hannah beseeching God for a son; David being hunted by Saul; Elijah fleeing from Jezebel and alone on the mountain; Nebuchadnezzar eating grass; Paul being smitten by blindness on the road to Damascus; and the list goes on. In fact, the more I thought about the men and women of scripture, the more I realized I couldn't recall any who did not endure trials and tribulations which changed them forever and brought them into a new relationship with God.

Pain as a Teacher

I too have learned pain is an effective teacher. David agrees. "Before I was afflicted I went astray, but now I keep your word." (Psalm 119:67). A few verses later he affirms the benefit of being afflicted. "It is good for me that I have been afflicted; That I may learn thy statutes." (Psalms 119:71)

I was hurting in ways I had only tasted in the past. I was completely unprepared for this event and I can't think of anything which would have helped me ahead of time. Having my world fall apart and then rebuild my relationship with God and my family has been the hardest and best journey I have ever been on. Suffering, pain, and brokenness are normal for Christians; in fact, Jesus says blessed are you if you mourn.

Prayer

While we admit we do not like painful experiences and would rather avoid being broken, we also acknowledge we grow and develop in the dark valleys of our soul. Thank you for being our Redeemer and working all things for our good. Thank you for being nearest, when we need you the most. Amen.

QUESTIONS FOR REFLECTION

1. Summarize how the summer of 2012 was for Steve. How did it illustrate the proverb, "Rome wasn't built in a day"?

2. Besides time, what did it take for Steve to change? What made him able to *"dig deeper and face [his] own pain and baggage"*?

3. Think about the analogy Steve used. With what did he compare his internal wounds and baggage?

4. What was and is a strong motivator for Steve to deal with his pain and baggage?

5. *"I have learned my past shapes me and contributes to my value system more than I ever fully comprehended....The past is always present, even when carefully concealed. Unless and until I acknowledge my pain and address my scars, I will wound the very people I am seeking to bless."* Do you agree with his analysis? Why or why not?

CHAPTER 7: BLESSED ARE THE BROKEN

Blessed

As I read through my Bible every year, I have favorite parts I look forward to where I savor each verse. I also have not-so-favorite sections which I read more quickly. One section in the latter category is the first few verses of the Beatitudes. "Blessed are the poor in spirit, for theirs is the kingdom of heaven. Blessed are those who mourn, for they shall be comforted." (Matthew 5:3-4)

I never had any desire to be poor in spirit or mourn. I didn't comprehend how the word "blessed" could be employed to describe people who were sad and mourning. How can it be a blessed experience to go through circumstances which leave me poor in spirit and hurting? But thanks to the experience of going through this difficult year, for the first time I am beginning to understand some of the blessings associated with being broken in spirit and mourning. (Brokenness can be defined as being needy, fragile, vulnerable, or wounded.)

Idiot Lights

Suffering and pain are similar to the lights on the dashboard of a car which signal there is a problem. When these lights begin to flash we can pull over to the side of the road and consult the driver's manual, or we can turn up the radio, put black tape over the offending light (I've heard of this being done), and pretend the problem doesn't exist. My mechanic friends call these flashing symbols "idiot lights" because by the time they come on it is often too late or the car is already having serious problems.

I am learning to heed the lights, or the gauges, on the dashboard of life, which represent hardship, pain, or suffering. These indicators need to be acknowledged and even embraced. They should not be covered up, ignored, or avoided. When I experienced my crisis, I didn't know how to fix my situation and I didn't have a manual. I had to acknowledge there was a problem and find help. The only thing I knew to do was ask 32 of my friends for help. Being this transparent was horrifying on one hand and wonderfully freeing on the other.

One of the things I learned over the course of the summer was being in a broken state freed me up from being concerned about what other people were thinking about me. I was needy and up against something bigger than myself, and I needed help. It was a relief to have "it" out in the open and not be pretending "it" didn't exist.

Reading directions and asking for help are hard for men, but necessary. Not only asking for help from my friends but enlisting the help of a professional therapist was not natural for me. I thought when I need advice with my taxes I consult my accountant. When I need legal advice I pay the big bucks for a lawyer. The same holds true for planning my financial future. How much more important is it to find out where my pain is coming from so I will not wound my wife and children with my own personal baggage.

Being broken made me more humble and teachable. I needed help and was desperate to learn how to love my wife, encourage my sons, and use words of encouragement to build them up instead of wounding them and crushing their spirits. Being cognizant of the suffering and pain I had caused led me to get the help I needed. It was hard to do, but today I look back with gratitude at the whole ordeal. I needed to change and God used this perfect storm to bring about lasting change.

Grace for the Needy

Being needy also qualified me for divine aid. God gives grace to the humble, is near to the brokenhearted, and takes thought for the poor and needy. God appreciates a broken spirit and a contrite heart.

- "God opposes the proud, but gives grace to the humble" (James 4:6).
- "The Lord is near to the brokenhearted and saves the crushed in spirit" (Psalm 34:18).
- "As for me, I am poor and needy, but the Lord takes thought for me" (Psalm 40:17).
- "The sacrifices of God are a broken spirit; a broken and contrite heart, O God, you will not despise" (Psalm 51:17).

His grace, plus a wake-up call from my family, combined to make changes which would not endure for only a few weeks or months but are still bearing good fruit several years later.

Slow to Speak and Careful to Listen

David was an authentic follower of God. He could have expunged the sordid tale of adultery, murder, lying, and cover-up over Uriah and Bathsheba. Instead the king of Israel, the man after God's own heart, left this sordid account in the chronicles of his kingdom for all to read. He even let us read his private journal about the experience in Psalm 51, where he acknowledges and confesses his sin and then asks God to rebuild him. Fortunately for us, David had a faithful friend named Nathan, who at the expense of his friendship and perhaps his own life, confronted him with the truth. David, to his credit, received the rebuke and became a new man.

My wife and sons took a risk speaking truth to me. Not being as rooted and grounded in God's love as I am now, I normally took correction badly and personally. On a lighter note, I once saw this quote on a plaque: "A psychiatrist will give you expensive advice that your wife can give you for free." My first thought when I read this clever saying was no one knows me better than my wife, and her advice and analysis of me have always been remarkably accurate. I need her input if I am to grow.

My second thought is the price of a professional consultation is steep and my wife can save me some money. But after I gave this more thought I recognized there is a price to pay for such insight, but it is not me who will pay for it. I think my wife will pay a terrific price if her advice is not received with humility and grace. I know more than ever I can shrivel my wife's spirit with a callous or sarcastic rejoinder. If I react badly when she gives me sound counsel, she will think twice before ever doing so again. I have been given a wonderful resource in my prudent wife who is "from the Lord." (Proverbs 19:14) May God help me to be prayerful and careful when asking her for wisdom.

I asked myself this question this morning: "Why am I writing this book?" I hope if there is another man in pain he will know he is not alone. I hope he will also find comfort in knowing most men need a crisis or wakeup call before they will acknowledge their need and get help. I am also hoping some readers will learn from my experience and not need a 911 experience or see the bombs dropping on Pearl Harbor before they open themselves up for deep healing and transformation. If you are in this latter category, kudos to you. Don't give up but stay the course; it is worth the effort.

I also hope someone reading this will have their eyes opened to the pain and suffering their own baggage is inflicting on those closest to them. I don't like pain in my own life and it hurts me to see others enduring hardship. Another reason I am writing this book is in the hope some impressionable children and tenderhearted women will be spared unnecessary hurt from their father and husband.

Bear One Another's Burden and So Fulfill the Law of Christ

Having carried a burden has enabled me to empathize with others' pain. I am able to tune in to what people are feeling more than ever. My own issues have helped me to understand what my brothers and sisters are experiencing in a new way. I observe pain everywhere. When I see people in some form of addiction, I don't see the outward behavior as much as I am cognizant of internal suffering. People do not hurt and abuse themselves for pleasure; there are reasons behind their actions. I am convinced I might have engaged in the same behaviors if I had walked in their shoes and grown up in their circumstances. Addiction takes many forms, some condemned by society (drugs, alcohol, pornography) and others rewarded (greed, power, success). But heartache and pain are often the reasons we do what we do. No one likes to hurt.

I find myself connecting with people in a deeper way because the one thing we all have in common is suffering. Whether we are battling our own issues or bearing the burden of someone we care for, we all need encouragement and support. When I reached out to those 32 friends and bared my heart and asked for help, it freed them up to also share their own hurts and griefs. We were connecting at a heart level and bearing each other's burdens in a healthy, godly way. Bearing each other's burdens and weeping with those who weep is Christianity at its best.

For a space of over a year I rarely had superficial conversations. When someone would ask how I was doing I would say, "Do you really want to know?" If they hesitated, I would say, "I'm doing," and let it go. But if they wanted to know, then I told them. It was wonderfully liberating to be honest and not lie by saying I was fine when I wasn't. I was able to be true to myself and not hide behind a fake mask. I am finding there is a hunger among God's people for candor, honesty, authenticity, and transparency.

One sister in Christ commented when we do have times in our church services for a life story or testimonial, it is normally a story of their life before Christ accompanied by tales of sordid sin and destructive behavior. Then they "come to Jesus" and their lives are forever changed. But how often have we heard from someone who has been a faithful Christian describe how they fell, were struggling or hurting, stand up and ask for help and support?

There are few quick fixes for any of the problems and sorrows of life. Life is a journey, and we are each bearing burdens. We need to be open with each other and receive the support of the body of Christ. When I sent out my email to my friends asking for help, I took a risk. How would they respond? Would they try to fix me? Would they judge me? Would they cut me off? Would I be asked to speak at their conventions in the future?

The more secure I have become in Christ, and the more comfortable in my own skin, the more I am willing to be open and transparent. What I have learned is once I share my story, others feel free to share their story, and we have connection, a mutual bond, and are able to share and bear one another's burdens. Nelson Mandela said, "As we let our own light shine, we unconsciously give other people permission to do the same." We all need encouragement, not only from the person of Christ in heaven but from the body of Christ on earth.

I have also observed in places where committed Christians congregate we are prone to share our successes but reticent to name our failures. It is permissible to ask for prayer for sickness, cancer, or some malady with a name and diagnosis. But what do you do if you and your children are being abused, or you are depressed, or you can't describe your condition but life just seems too big and you need emotional support and encouragement?

And God forbid you have a problem and it doesn't go away in one volley of faith-filled prayer or one church-wide coordinated effort to supply meals to your family! Perhaps you have a family member affected by a life-changing disability, or a victim of a stroke that has been left partially paralyzed, or any one of several long-term needs which will not change.

When we learn to bear each other's burdens, truly care for each other, give grace to each other, and sit beside one another, we will be fulfilling the law of Christ. In the process of acknowledging we are all frail, needy humans, with strengths and weaknesses, and love each other as Jesus has loved us, we will have a wonderful impact on our neighbors as well. "By this all people will know that you are my disciples, if you have love for one another" (John 13:35).

Prayer

Knowing that in you we live and move and have our being, help us to count it all joy when we meet trials of various kinds. Thank you for being near to us when are brokenhearted and crushed in spirit. (adapted from Acts 17:28, James 1:2, Psalm 34:18)

QUESTIONS FOR REFLECTION

1. Write the verses in Matthew that fell under the "not-so-favorite" category for Steve as he read through the Bible each year. Define brokenness.

2. Being "broken" led to what positive results for Steve? What other positive fruits could emerge from being broken?

3. Steve asks himself why he is writing this book. Can you summarize his reasons?

4. What addictive behaviors are rewarded in our society? Do you agree? Explain. Also, what has been your experience with any of these addictive behaviors, either in yourself or in someone you know?

5. What has Steve seen happen when he shares his story? Have you experienced that?

CHAPTER 8: KNOWING GOD AND SERVING GOD

The Trinity

Through this period of sorrow I came to know the difference between serving God and knowing Him. I just wanted the pain to stop and life to return to normal. Thankfully, God gave me even more than I sought, for I am learning more about the nature and personhood of God. I had fervently served God for decades, but in this crisis I came to know God Himself in a new way. I am trying to find the words to describe the qualitative difference in my relationship with the living God. When I take time to be still and draw near, I draw near to my Dad(God the Father), my Brother (God the Son), and my Friend (God the Spirit). God is three persons who are different and special each in their own uniqueness. Yet they are also one. While they are all God, they are not just a distant, eternal, omnipotent being, but members of the Trinity I have come to know.

Knowing God is the reason we live. Paul wanted to know Christ above all else. Paul did all he could to build and establish the church, but his real motivation was to know God. "I count all things to be loss for the excellency of the knowledge of Christ Jesus my Lord: for whom I suffered the loss of all things, and do count them but refuse, that I may gain Christ, and be found in him, not having a

righteousness of mine own, even that which is of the law, but that which is through faith in Christ, the righteousness which is from God by faith" (Philippians 3:8–9).

Moses wanted to know God more than he wanted to lead the children of Israel out of the wilderness or see the promised land. "Moses said to the LORD, 'See, you say to me, "Bring up this people," but you have not let me know whom you will send with me. Yet you have said, "I know you by name, and you have also found favor in my sight." Now therefore, if I have found favor in your sight, please show me now your ways, that I may know you in order to find favor in your sight. Consider too that this nation is your people.' And he said, 'My presence will go with you, and I will give you rest.' And he said to him, 'If your presence will not go with me, do not bring us up from here'" (Exodus 33:12–14). Notice the phrase in verse 13: "show me now your ways, that I may know you." This is what motivated Moses.

The Father, My Dad

I don't want to be casual with God the Father Almighty, but when I read He is my Abba, then I think it is fitting I call Him Dad. I believe the desire to have a Dad who understands us completely and loves us for who we are is built into our hearts. We get glimpses and tastes of this kind of care and affection from our earthly fathers, but we are only complete when His Spirit makes us know He is our Daddy (Romans 8:15). As I grow in this relationship, my deepest heart needs are being met by the best Dad ever, my eternal Father.

We were made for Him. Since His love and affection have made fresh inroads into my heart "through the Holy Spirit" (Romans 5:5), my life has been deeply enriched. I look forward to being quiet and still in His presence. I love being with Him. I love my Dad, and my Dad loves me.

The Spirit

I rarely am fully engaged when the closing benediction is read, because it sounds like church-speak and is filled with words like grace and peace. But this particular morning these words spoke to my heart with new meaning. "The grace of the Lord Jesus Christ and the love of God and the fellowship of the Holy Spirit be with you all" (2 Corinthians 13:14). During my recent journey, I have been appreciating the grace of Jesus and how He died for me while I was a sinner. I have also been comprehending the love of God and how much He likes me for who I am, not what I do.

The choice of words in the last portion of the verse are what especially caught my attention: "the fellowship of the Holy Spirit." Fellowship is also rendered communion or presence in other translations. I have heard about the power, conviction, or inspiration of the Spirit, but this language suggests the third person of the Trinity is indeed a person with whom I can enjoy the fellowship of His presence. As I pondered this concept, my mind was drawn to a few scriptures which shed more light on the person of the Spirit and tied in to what I had been learning.

"God's love has been poured into our hearts through the Holy Spirit who has been given to us" (Romans 5:5). The Holy Spirit has a role in understanding and receiving the love of God. I knew the Spirit brought conviction and was responsible for bringing me to Jesus, but this verse showed me how He had been at the forefront when I asked God to help me love Him with all my heart, soul, mind, and strength. It was the Holy Spirit who poured the love of God into my heart.

In John 14:16 I read, "I will pray the Father, and he shall give you another Comforter, that he may be with you for ever." In my sorrow the Comforter had been at my side. I was never alone, for He will never leave me. I know this sounds elementary, and it is, but Jesus is not on earth any longer. He is sitting at the right hand of the Father interceding for us. When Jesus ascended, He ascended into heaven. But the Helper was sent to help us. "Nevertheless, I tell you the truth: it is to your advantage that I go away, for if I do not go away, the Helper will not come to you. But if I go, I will send him to you" (John 16:7). I am learning to know and have a relationship with the good Spirit who is with me forever.

Knowing the Son as the Man of Sorrows

Through this difficult time I also came to know the Man of Sorrows in a deep way. Jesus is described in Isaiah 53 as a man of sorrows and acquainted with grief. He is also meek, gentle, and lowly of heart. He was the suffering messiah, the sacrificial lamb, who was bruised, crushed, beaten, pierced, and smitten for our sin. He was a broken man who bore our griefs and carried our sorrows.

I sensed His presence when I was hurting. I became almost comfortable with suffering, because He was there and I had a small taste of who He was and what He was like. I did not mind being in a valley because Jesus lives in valleys. He is a "very present help in trouble" and "acquainted with grief." Experiencing the presence and compassion of the Spirit of Jesus helped take the sting out of my momentary trial.

I am even learning to appreciate and understand the first two Beatitudes, which I used to read through quickly. I did not have any desire to mourn or be poor in spirit, but Jesus said people in this state are blessed! I am beginning to understand the good fruit of mourning is being comforted—by Him. And being blessed when poor in spirit is not attractive because you possess the kingdom of heaven but because you possess the King Himself.

I have also observed Jesus enjoyed an incredible relationship with His Father. He also was filled, led, and dependent on the Holy Spirit. He invested time and energy in understanding the truth as revealed in scripture. All of the preparation and training which took place in the first 30 years of the life of Jesus was equipping Him to die. He came to die. He was born to die. The pure, spotless Son of God died so we might live. His death broke the power of sin and hell and ushered in new life. But Jesus is not the only one who must die. If I am to be His follower, I must die as well. "He said to all, 'If anyone would come after me, let him deny himself and take up his cross daily and follow me'" (Luke 9:23).

Prayer

"The grace of the Lord Jesus Christ and the love of God and the fellowship of the Holy Spirit be with you all." (2 Corinthians 13:14)

QUESTIONS FOR REFLECTION

1. What motivated and constrained Paul?

2. How did Moses learn more about the character of God?

3. Are you comfortable calling your Heavenly Father Dad or Daddy? Why or why not?

4. Name some attributes of the "fellowship of the Holy Spirit" from the scriptures in this chapter.

5. What is the best part of being in a valley of suffering? Explain.

CHAPTER 9: EMBRACE THE CROSS

Surrender

If I were to name the single most significant change which has improved our family relationships over the last three years, I would say I died. This is one of the central points of this book. The more I assimilated the love of God, walked with the Spirit, and comprehended the wonderful grace of Jesus, the better prepared I was to surrender, let go, and die.

There has been a significant life-altering difference between past crises and this one. The transformation has been tangible and deep and it occurred in my own heart. My family and I are experiencing really good fruit in our relationships with one another. Fruit comes from seeds dying. "'Truly, truly, I say to you, unless a grain of wheat falls into the earth and dies, it remains alone; but if it dies, it bears much fruit'" (John 12:24).

I attribute this to an attitude shift, a dying to myself, in a way I have never done before. The heart is where change occurs, but it is difficult to measure or even describe. I am going to try to explain what has occurred using specific examples and scriptures which God has brought to mind.

As a husband, father, pastor, speaker, and businessman, I tried to do it all. I don't think I consciously avoided dying, but when an issue would arise, instead of stopping and considering the root issue, I simply worked harder so I would not have to think it through and change. Perhaps I was simply lazy and wanted to beat the system. I put a significant effort into being a good husband and father. I always want to learn new strategies and techniques. I understand now God is not calling for more and better, but He is calling for me to surrender, take His yoke, and die.

Temporary Changes Are Not Dying

When Moses entreated Pharaoh to let the Israelites go, Pharaoh endured one plague after another and eventually would give in and offer to let the people go. But when the plague would subside, he would change his mind and not release them. You would think any one of the disasters of that magnitude would make him want to repent and release the Israelites. But we know it took ten plagues, including the loss of his firstborn son, before he finally reached the breaking point. How I resonate with Pharaoh on this point. Many times I would need to change and would repent for a season and be different, but eventually I would revert to my old habits and way of living. I would still be the same old guy.

Sacrifice Is Not Dying

There is a similar theme found in the life of Saul. One of the most convicting accounts in the Bible to me is when Saul lost his kingship. The whole story is recorded in 1 Samuel 15. Saul was commanded to completely destroy the Amalekites because of the way they treated the Israelites as they came up out of Egypt. But instead, Saul gave in to the wishes of the people and smote the Amalekites but spared Agag the king and kept the best of the cattle and goods. Samuel rebukes him in verse 22, "Has the LORD as great delight in burnt offerings and sacrifices, as in obeying the voice of the LORD? Behold, to obey is better than sacrifice." Bottom line, Saul was not obedient, and this event lost him his throne. God gave a simple, clear, direct command, and Saul disobeyed. God is not looking for sacrifices but obedience. I know I can make sacrifices for a season and seem to change, but still be the same egg.

The Old Testament was written "for our instruction" (1 Corinthians 10:11). Saul was a troubled man. As I read the account of his life in 1 Samuel, I identify with him at many points. He took input from even his most trusted advisors and family, personally. He wanted to please God but also sought to please the people. He had a spiritual side, but he also had pain and personal demons. When stressed, he lashed out at his son Jonathan and threw a spear at him in his own home.

Saul also genuinely repented for his mishaps. On many occasions while pursuing David in the wilderness, He would sincerely apologize to David when his life was spared, but within a short time, he was chasing David as before. My behavior was cyclical as well. It seems that regardless of the changes Saul wanted to make, he continued to revert to his default settings. I thought of him when I read this verse in Job 14:22, "He feels only the pain of his own body, and he mourns only for himself."

Since Sandi and I have begun to process what we learned through this difficult time, I asked her what changes she thought I had made which had improved our relationship. Her observation was; when I read a book or attended a seminar I would be teachable and change for a time, but there was no deep, lasting transformation. When the crisis first occurred in the spring of 2012, I desperately sought to understand myself and this pain and learned a lot in a short period of time. I found a letter I wrote in May of 2012 and it was totally accurate. I acknowledged my sins as a husband and was very specific.

If she had forgiven me and moved back home, I believe I would have been a semi-changed man for a few months or even longer. If I had been able to hold my breath and make some sacrifices for a season, there would not have been the long-term, lasting, internal transformation that I am currently experiencing. I needed to die and not make temporary modifications to my behavior. At the time, I could not understand why this difficult season was taking so long. I am generally a quick learner. Through reflection, study, therapy, and treatment, I had figured out what to do. I had thrown myself into the process and surmised that now that I understood we could be a normal family again.

I now see I would not have died to the same degree I have if the program had been short circuited by my persistent and poignant appeals. I needed time to go deeper and make lasting changes. She needed time to breathe and be healed. She needed time to rebuild trust. Most of the summer, I believed I had too much time to think and feel. Now I recognize I had just the right amount of time.

I heard a similar theme recently when a woman described years of pain and abuse which led her to Christ. She said she was thankful for her past, all of it, because she would not be where she was or who she was without the pain and the suffering. She then illustrated her point with the story of a butterfly. When a well-meaning person comes upon a caterpillar striving to emerge from its cocoon, his first thought is to relieve the pain and help the struggling larva be free. But to do so would cripple the caterpillar. The process of escaping from the silky envelope, the struggle to be liberated from the confines of the cocoon, is what develops the strength in the wings which equips the butterfly to soar and fly.

Over the years, when we would have a problem in our relationship, Sandi would buy another book on marriage which would exhort her to be more respectful, more submissive, and more attractive. Or she would go to an older, godly woman who would encourage her to simply press on and endure the best she could. Wherever she turned, the theme was the same: she needed to make changes. If she did the marriage would be helped. As a result, Sandi blamed herself and lived in shame, thinking our relationship was suffering because of her failure to change.

Several years ago, a good friend had recommended a book to me which had changed his life. I read it and then Sandi did. It is called Discovering the Mind of a Woman by Ken Nair. I have since met Ken and his wife, attended their seminar, and counseled with them. They are the real deal. After reading the book, Sandi remarked this was the only book she had encountered calling for the husband to die and change. I got the same message. My wife was not the problem here, I was. I did not want to die. I thought I could simply try harder and do better. I knew what my responsibilities were as a Christian husband. I had written about them and taught seminars on the role of the man for over a decade.

In 2012, I knew I could no longer dodge, make sacrifices, or temporarily be different, I had to die.

Why Die?

One motivation for choosing to die and not keep making temporary changes or sacrifices was seeing the impact my own stuff had on my family. I will never know what each member of my family has gone through. But the few insights I have gleaned are so hard to comprehend I can hardly process them. I hate being hurt and perhaps because I have tasted the awfulness of being wounded by those you love, I loathe doing the same thing to those I love.

I also came within a whisker of losing my wife, and having my children move away. When I was a young boy my younger brothers began to forbid me to play with their toys. As one of them said, "You always break our toys." I did not set out to break them but was curious what would happen if you wound it the mechanism 25 times instead of the recommended 24. The only way to know, is to wind it until it breaks.

I found the breaking point for my family in April, 2012. I never want to go near this edge again.

Take Up the Cross

For me to be obedient to God's call, I had to take up my cross daily and die. I needed to lay my life down for my wife and love her as Christ loved the Church. He died for the Church. I also recognize my wife and children were the ones who were dying all those years when I would descend into a dark place, tired, stressed, or worn out. They had been paying the price for my unwillingness to face my own stuff and get help. I have also begun to see God did not call them or create them to die. I am the one who was designed to die. I am called to lay my life down for my wife and family. I am to follow Jesus and love them as He loved me and laid His life down so I could live. My wife is designed to respect and submit. My children are designed to honor and obey. I was created, called, and designed to die. I recognize we all need to die to self and take up our cross, but men are specifically commanded to lay their life down for their wife.

I don't want this concept to be theoretical so I have given specific examples of areas where I let go and in a sense died. Concerning the business, I died to having the final say, having control, having veto power, holding the purse strings, and being the majority shareholder. Until I let these things go completely, signed the papers and finalized the agreement, I hadn't died. I have shared how hard this was for me, but it had to happen for our family to move on. I had said I would follow this course of action and now I had to be true to what I said, quit waffling, be a man, and follow though.

At one point a good friend reminded me of the scripture "He that swears to his own hurt." This verse is found in Psalm 15 and describes those who were to dwell in God's holy hill. "O LORD, who shall sojourn in your tent? Who shall dwell on your holy hill? ... He who swears to his own hurt and does not change" (Psalm 15:1, 4). I had been remembering the same verse and this was a confirmation God wanted me to let go, even if it hurt, because I had said I would. This was a dying experience.

The Old Cross and the New, by A. W. Tozer

The following excerpts are taken from *Man: The Dwelling Place of God* is an anointed essay by a godly author. If you have never read anything by

Tozer I recommend *The Pursuit of God and The Knowledge of the Holy*.

ALL UNANNOUNCED AND MOSTLY UNDETECTED there has come in modern times a new cross into popular evangelical circles. It is like the old cross, but different: the likenesses are superficial; the differences, fundamental.

The old cross would have no truck with the world. For Adam's proud flesh it meant the end of the journey. It carried into effect the sentence imposed by the law of Sinai. The new cross is not opposed to the human race; rather, it is a friendly pal and, if understood aright, it is the source of oceans of good clean fun and innocent enjoyment. It lets Adam live without interference. His life motivation is unchanged; he still lives for his own pleasure, only now he takes delight in singing choruses and watching religious movies instead of singing bawdy songs and drinking hard liquor. The accent is still on enjoyment, though the fun is now on a higher plane morally if not intellectually.

The new cross encourages a new and entirely different evangelistic approach. The evangelist does not demand abnegation of the old life before a new life can be received. He preaches not contrasts but similarities. He seeks to key into public interest by showing that Christianity makes no unpleasant demands; rather, it offers the same thing the world does, only on a higher level. Whatever the sin-mad world happens to be clamoring after at the moment is cleverly shown to be the very thing the gospel offers, only the religious product is better.

The new cross does not slay the sinner, it redirects him. It gears him into a cleaner and jollier way of living and saves his self-respect. To the self-assertive it says, "Come and assert yourself for Christ." To the egotist it says, "Come and do your boasting in the Lord." To the thrill seeker it says, "Come and enjoy the thrill of Christian fellowship." The Christian message is slanted in the direction of the current vogue in order to make it acceptable to the public.

The philosophy back of this kind of thing may be sincere but its sincerity does not save it from being false. It misses completely the whole meaning of the cross.

The old cross is a symbol of death. It stands for the abrupt, violent end of a human being. The man in Roman times who took up his cross and started down the road had already said good-by to his friends. He was not coming back. He was going out to have it ended. The cross made no compromise, modified nothing, spared nothing; it slew all of the man, completely and for good. It did not try to keep on good terms with its victim. It struck cruel and hard, and when it had finished its work, the man was no more.

God offers life, but not an improved old life. The life He offers is life out of death. It stands always on the far side of the cross. Whoever would possess it must pass under the rod. He must repudiate himself and concur in God's just sentence against him.

What does this mean to the individual, the condemned man who would find life in Christ Jesus? He must forsake his sins and then go on to forsake himself. Let him cover nothing, defend nothing, excuse nothing.

Having done this let him gaze with simple trust upon the risen Savior, and from Him will come life and rebirth and cleansing and power. The cross that ended the earthly life of Jesus now puts an end to the sinner; and the power that raised Christ from the dead now raises him to a new life along with Christ. (A. W.

Tozer, Man, The Dwelling Place of God, 1966)

"For the word of the cross is to those who are perishing foolishness, but to us who are being saved it is the power of God." (1 Corinthians 1:18)

"Then Jesus said to His disciples, "If anyone wishes to come after Me, let him deny himself, and take up his cross, and follow Me. "For whoever wishes to save his life shall lose it; but whoever loses his life for My sake shall find it." (Matthew 16:24-25 NASB)

All God's plans have the mark of the cross on them, and all His plans have death to self in them. --E. M Bounds

Joint Heirs

In the home, which is now made up of Sandi, John, and myself, I died to being in charge of the joint bank account. We have divvied up our financial responsibilities, which is important to Sandi, and so I acquiesced to her desire to have her own account.

It was hard for me to acknowledge we jointly owned the business. In my mind, I thought of it as my business even though she was a contributor. In my mind I did the lion's share of the work and put in the most hours directly building the business. Therefore I should have the largest share of our assets. This is not fun to write, but it is true. We have worked through this issue, and I am comfortable recognizing it has been "our" business all along, for we are truly one flesh.

I no longer have the final say on where we are to worship. We have found a church where we are each comfortable. It is a compromise of sorts as it would not be the first choice for either of us, but we are working together as a team and sometimes we each have to give in to find a middle ground.

There were other areas I needed to release. They were more subtle, but just as real, and had certainly been felt by my wife and sons. These were deeply held beliefs and attitudes which affected our marriage relationship and roles. One of these attitudes was how I viewed my wife. Deep down, I believed since my wife was my helpmeet, and she was to be submissive, this translated into treating her as a second-class citizen. I didn't know I was doing this until she told me. But when it was brought to my attention I saw it for what it was. Scripture teaches we are joint heirs. We may have differing roles, but we are most certainly equal before God, and if anything I should serve her and treat her better than myself "Do nothing from selfish ambition or conceit, but in humility count others more significant than yourselves." (Philippians 2:3)

Serve

Even though Jesus taught the difference between rulers in this world and rulers in the kingdom of God, I didn't apply this truth in my home. "You know that the rulers of the Gentiles lord it over them, and their great ones exercise authority over them. It shall not be so among you. But whoever would be great among you must be your servant." (Matthew 20:25-26) I reasoned that since that since I was the head of the home, my work (business and ministry) was the most important activity in the family. When I needed help unloading a truck or filling orders or shipping product or meeting a deadline, I expected the family to drop what they were doing and pitch in. These were not always bad activities, as I tried to make it fun and rewarding, but when you add them all up, they paint a picture of a man who is king of his castle.

As king, I expected to have my meals prepared, my laundry done, and the house cleaned, with very little help from me. This has drastically changed and I help out a good deal around the house. My helping out holds deep meaning for Sandi, as I have found out by asking. When I do the dishes, wash clothes, clean up the kitchen, or prepare meals, she feels like the work which she has done for 35-plus years is valued and appreciated, not taken for granted.

I am trying to be as specific as possible to help you see the difference in our family dynamic. In addition to having two bank accounts and my helping around the house more, we have divided up John's care between the two of us so it does not all fall on her shoulders.

One of the hardest places for me to let go was always being right. I think I remembered certain events one way but others had a different recollection. Unless something is uber important I am learning to let it go. If I need more information, I am learning to ask a question for clarification. Then after some honest discussion, be willing to agree to disagree if necessary. I am still working on this but even considering it is major progress.

I have listed a few tangible applications but recognize different activities may resonate differently for each marriage. The bottom line is dying to my expectations and taking the attitude of a servant has certainly blessed my bride.

This is consistent with Paul's exhortation to have the mindset of Jesus, which is much different than mine was. "Do nothing from selfish ambition or conceit, but in humility count others more significant than yourselves. Let each of you look not only to his own interests, but also to the interests of others. Have this mind among yourselves, which is yours in Christ Jesus, who, though he was in the form of God, did not count equality with God a thing to be grasped, but emptied himself, by taking the form of a servant, being born in the likeness of men. And being found in human form, he humbled himself by becoming obedient to the point of death, even death on a cross" (Philippians 2:3-8).

Help in Dying

The Spirit of God helps us. He is called the Helper. These two passages point to His assistance in moving from making sacrifices and short term changes to long term transformation and dying. I do not know how He operates, and I can't point to a specific instance when He worked for me, but I know He did. "For if you live according to the flesh you will die, but if by the Spirit you put to death the deeds of the body, you will live." (Romans 8:13)

When Jesus was wrestling and seeking to commit to the course God had given to Him, He seat drops of blood and finally after agonizing prayer, He submitted to the plan of God and said, "My Father, if it be possible, let this cup pass from me; nevertheless, not as I will, but as you will." (Matthew 26:39). I think this was when our salvation was secured. When Jesus embraced the cross and committed to die. I also think the Eternal Spirit of God helped Him. "How much more will the blood of Christ, who through the eternal Spirit offered himself without blemish to God, purify our conscience from dead works to serve the living God." (Hebrews 9:14)

Not only have I found my life by losing it, I am also seeing better fruit. "Truly, truly, I say to you, unless a grain of wheat falls into the earth and dies, it remains alone; but if it dies, it bears much fruit." (John 12:24)

Prayer

May the same Eternal Spirit who enabled Jesus to say, "nevertheless, not my will, but thine, be done" (Luke 22:42), help us to die, so we can live. For Jesus promised "Whoever finds his life will lose it, and whoever loses his life for my sake will find it." (Matthew 10:39)

QUESTIONS FOR REFLECTION

1. Do you identify with the distinction between long-term dying and short-term sacrifices?

2. Explain Saul's cyclical behavior.

3. If you are a husband, what is your response Ken Nair's book calling for the husband to die and change? (If this is a challenging idea for you, consider obtaining and reading a copy of *Discovering the Mind of a Woman*.)

4. What are children called to do? What are wives called to do? What are husbands called to do?

5. What are some practical areas where Steve learned to die? Husbands, what are some areas where **you** need to die?

CHAPTER 10: ROOTED AND GROUNDED

Ephesus

About the same time I was being edified by John 15:9 I was also contemplating the Ephesian church. In Revelation 2 they were told they had lost their first love. I then read the Letter to the Ephesians with new eyes. There are wonderful words of grace in Ephesians which inspire love for God "By grace you have been saved through faith. And this is not your own doing; it is the gift of God." (Ephesians 2:8) The inspired prayer Paul recorded for these believers who struggled with maintaining their first love stood out to me the most. I hope you will read it prayerfully and slowly as it is one of the most inspired prayers for those of us who want to comprehend God's love more.

"For this reason I bow my knees before the Father, from whom every family in heaven and on earth is named, that according to the riches of His glory he may grant you to be strengthened with power through His Spirit in your inner being, so that Christ may dwell in your hearts through faith—that you, being rooted and grounded in love, may have strength to comprehend with all the saints what is the breadth and length and height and depth, and to know the love of Christ that surpasses knowledge, that you may be filled with all the fullness of God.

Now to Him who is able to do far more abundantly than all that we ask or think, according to the power at work within us, to him be glory in the church and in Christ Jesus throughout all generations, forever and ever. Amen." (Ephesians 3:14–21)

Right in the middle of this passage are these words: "rooted and grounded in love," and they are followed soon after by "to know the love of Christ that surpasses knowledge." These words, "rooted and grounded in love," resonate in my heart. I find myself asking, How can I do this? What can I do to work with God's good Spirit to be rooted and grounded in the love of Christ? I know the Holy Spirit plays an important role in this process because of Romans 5:5: "God's love has been poured into our hearts through the Holy Spirit who has been given to us."

I believe being rooted and grounded in the love of Christ is the most fundamental truth for Christians to apply for the following reasons:

1. The more I comprehend and assimilate the "breadth and length and height and depth" of the love of God, the more I am empowered and stirred to love Him, which is the first and greatest commandment. "We love because He first loved us" (1 John 4:19). The more we are loved, the more we love. The more love we receive from God, the more love we give to God.

2. The more love I receive, the more I am equipped to love my neighbor as myself. All the other commands flow from these two commands.

3. Jesus says, "Love one another as I have loved you" (John 15:12). I am limited in my ability to love others if I haven't tasted "as I have loved you." To the degree I have been loved, to the same degree I am able to love. I can only give what I have received. "He that is forgiven much loves much" (Luke 7:41 -47).

I don't want to keep quoting this scripture until you are numb to its efficacy, but this is the fundamental truth upon which all relationships in the kingdom of God are based. Whether it is loving God, loving my neighbor, or loving my wife, the quality of my love for each of them is dependent on how much love I have received and apprehended. This wonderful journey of being loved by God begins with God Himself and the good news of the gospel. Absorbing this basic and yet sublime truth of God's affection for me will determine how well I am able to love God and others.

The Good Fruit from Being Rooted in God's Love

My point in writing this section of the book is to show how being rooted in God's love impacts every area of my life. Following loving God, my overwhelming desire is to love my wife and children. I have written a book focusing on how God is helping me to love my wife and children as He loves me called *Transformed in Love*. Every point in this book flows from first being immersed, secured, and established in God's love for me. Here are a few examples of how my role as a husband and father is transformed by meditating on and experiencing how God is a husband and father to me.

As Christ Loved Me, I Am to Love My Wife

As a husband I am commanded to love my wife as Christ loved the church, or as Christ loved me. "Husbands, love your wives, as Christ loved the church and gave himself up for her" (Ephesians 5:25). This verse is clearly a restating of John 15:9 and 12. By meditating on how Jesus has loved me, I am helped to know how to love my wife.

For example, Jesus taught His disciples they were not to rule over one another but serve each other. "Whoever would be first among you must be your slave, even as the Son of Man came not to be served but to serve, and to give his life as a ransom for many" (Matthew 20:27-28).

Jesus taught this lesson in Matthew, and illustrated it in John 13. "When he had washed their feet and put on his outer garments and resumed his place, he said to them, "Do you understand what I have done to you? You call me Teacher and Lord, and you are right, for so I am. If I then, your Lord and Teacher, have washed your feet, you also ought to wash one another's feet. For I have given you an example, that you also should do just as I have done to you" (John 13:12-15).

As a husband, my role is not to be the king of my castle. My wife and children were not created to serve me, I have been designed to serve them. By meditating on how Jesus loved me by serving me, I follow His example and do not treat my wife and children as second-class citizens but as fellow children of God who were created in the image of God.

As My Heavenly Father Loves Me, I Am to Love My Children

God created and called me as a dad to teach His precepts diligently to my children and talk of them when I sit in my house, when I walk by the way, when I lie down, and when I rise (see Deuteronomy 11:19). But as we observed before, the prerequisite to teaching children to love God and His Word is for the parent teacher to love God and His Word himself.

The more I grasp how much God loves me, the more my love for God increases. The more I love Him, the better equipped I am to encourage my children to love God. We catch a fire from someone who has a fire. When I truly love God with all that is within me and am not lukewarm but fervently loving God, others will catch that fire themselves. As a parent I influence my children not just by my talk and my teaching, but by my walk as well. The more my walk matches my talk, the more likely my message will be received by those most dear to me.

As My Dad Likes Me, I Am to Love Myself

I hesitate to write this, but knowing God likes me has helped me to like myself. I know "no one ever hated his own flesh" (Ephesians 5:29), but I did not value myself until I began to grasp my heavenly Dad did. I am learning to see myself through His eyes instead of my own.

I have had trouble taking care of myself and rarely made time for Steve to rest, relax, and enjoy life. I recognize I have ascetic tendencies and lean towards a radical Saint Francis lifestyle. Knowing God values me gives me permission to embrace a more balanced outlook on life, recognizing God "richly provides us with everything to enjoy" (1 Timothy 6:17). When I do take care of my body, the temple of the Holy Spirit, I am much nicer to be around, kinder, gentler, and more loving. I am learning to rest when I am tired, make time to enjoy people and things, and relax. In other words, believing the good news is bearing good fruit in my relationship with my wife and kids.

Prayer

Help us God to love, as we have been loved. Open our eyes to how you have loved us and teach us how to love our spouses and children in the same fashion. Help us to be daily rooted and grounded in love, so we may have strength to comprehend with all the saints what is the breadth and length and height and depth, and to know the love of Christ that surpasses knowledge, that we may be filled with all the fullness of God. (Adapted from Ephesians 3:17–19)

QUESTIONS FOR REFLECTION

1. This chapter begins with *"one of the most inspired prayers for those of us who want to comprehend God's love more."* If you desire to mine the richness of this prayer, write or type Ephesians 3:16–21 and post it in your home or car where you can read and meditate on it daily. Choose small "bites" of it to chew on and pray through at one sitting, asking the Spirit to teach you.

2. What is the most fundamental truth for Christians to apply, in Steve's estimation? Why? How well have you applied it in your life?

3. Husbands: What are some ways Christ loved the church, or Christ loved you?

4. Loving your children and loving yourself: what resonates with you in the last two sections of this chapter? If something catches your attention, explore it further.

5. How has Steve's everyday behavior been changed by grasping more deeply his heavenly Dad's love for him?

CHAPTER 11:
LET GOD LOVE YOU

Crawling Up into God's Lap

Each morning when my son awakes, he comes downstairs and finds me. If I am standing he hugs me; if I am sitting he crawls into my lap. His hugs are more like holds, for he clings to me for an extended time. But whether standing or sitting, he first finds his dad and we hold each other. In this simple act we are communicating we love each other. We have been doing this for many years, and it is a wonderful way to begin each day.

In the same way, I need to look for God each morning and let Him hold me and love me and make me know that I am His kid. God certainly is our Dad and His love does not change, but I am learning that I have to take some initiative and get close to Him. Relationships are always a two-way street. Of course it is much easier for me to draw near to God knowing that He enjoys my presence.

In the past I may have been more like the shy schoolboy tentatively moving in His direction, looking down, scuffing my shoes, afraid to meet His eyes. But then I looked up and saw that He was smiling. This morning I was rereading the account of the return of the prodigal son. "I will arise and go to my father, and I will say to him, 'Father, I have sinned against heaven and before you. I am no longer worthy to be called your son. Treat me as one of your hired servants.' And he arose and came to his father. But while he was still a long way off, his father saw him and felt compassion, and ran and embraced him and kissed him. And the son said to him, 'Father, I have sinned against heaven and before you. I am no longer worthy to be called your son.' But the father said to his servants, 'Bring quickly the best robe, and put it on him, and put a ring on his hand, and shoes on his feet. And bring the fattened calf and kill it, and let us eat and celebrate. For this my son was dead, and is alive again; he was lost, and is found.' And they began to celebrate" (Luke 15:18-24).

I love this picture of the father who had compassion, ran, embraced, and kissed his son. The son was trying to make his little speech of repentance, and his dad interrupted him, grabbed him, and gave him a bear hug. This is our Dad too. (Recently I had a friend point out where God may be giving us each a hug in scripture, in Psalm 139:5: "You hem me in, behind and before, and lay your hand upon me." Whether this is accurate or not, in the past two years when I have drawn near to Him I have found He is always smiling, always loving, and always welcoming.

Knocking and Whispering

Another image in scripture is of God standing at the door and knocking. He is doing His part in reaching out to us but is behind a closed door. It is our part to open the door and invite Him in. This passage has often been incorrectly applied to God seeking the lost and the unsaved. But these are not unbelievers God is seeking, but His own people. They are still following Him, but at a distance. Our Dad desires to be close to us. He wants to share our life with us, but we have the opportunity and the responsibility to open the door and let Him in.

"Behold, I stand at the door and knock. If anyone hears my voice and opens the door, I will come in to him and eat with him, and he with me" (Revelation 3:20). If God is knocking and you hear His still small voice whispering to your heart, then open the door and invite Him in. "Seek the LORD while he may be found; call upon him while he is near" (Isaiah 55:6). "So the LORD must wait for you to come to him so he can show you his love and compassion. For the LORD is a faithful God. Blessed are those who wait for his help." (Isaiah 30:18 NLT)

Be Still and Know

I am choosing to invest time soaking in the presence of God and reveling in the truth of God's love. As the truth of God liking me for who I am, not what I do, lodges deep in my heart and mind, I am being transformed. Transformation and change take time and intentionality. The more I comprehend the unconditional love of God, the better equipped I am to give this same kind of love and fulfill the new commandment. For he says in John 13:34, "A new commandment I give to you, that you love one another: just as I have loved you."

Since the word I have used the most in this section is "rooted," consider the parable of the sower. " 'A sower went out to sow his seed. And as he sowed, some fell along the path and was trampled underfoot, and the birds of the air devoured it. And some fell on the rock, and as it grew up, it withered away, because it had no moisture. And some fell among thorns, and the thorns grew up with it and choked it. And some fell into good soil and grew and yielded a hundredfold.' As he said these things, he called out, 'He who has ears to hear, let him hear.'

"And when his disciples asked him what this parable meant, he said, 'To you it has been given to know the secrets of the kingdom of God, but for others they are in parables, so that "seeing they may not see, and hearing they may not understand." Now the parable is this: The seed is the word of God. The ones along the path are those who have heard; then the devil comes and takes away the word from their hearts, so that they may not believe and be saved. And the ones on the rock are those who, when they hear the word, receive it with joy. But these have no root; they believe for a while, and in time of testing fall away. And as for what fell among the thorns, they are those who hear, but as they go on their way they are choked by the cares and riches and pleasures of life, and their fruit does not mature. As for that in the good soil, they are those who, hearing the word, hold it fast in an honest and good heart, and bear fruit with patience'" (Luke 8:5–15).

If you are still reading, you obviously are hungry and have "ears to hear." Those who "hear the Word" also "hold it fast," guarding it from being stolen by the devil. They are not shallow but have depth to endure testing, and they nurture the seeds so they are not "choked by the cares and riches and pleasures of life." They care about the truth. On one hand, they guard against losing it, and on the other they invest time and energy to cultivate the truth until it bears good fruit. Deepening roots takes time, regular watering, and patience. But good fruit follows.

We in the western world are all about working harder to get better results, yet we are limited in our understanding of many images in scripture since they are set in an agricultural community. Working harder does not produce more fruit. According to John, abiding in Christ precedes bearing fruit for Christ. "'Abide in me, and I in you. As the branch cannot bear fruit by itself, unless it abides in the vine, neither can you, unless you abide in me. I am the vine; you are the branches. Whoever abides in me and I in him, he it is that bears much fruit, for apart from me you can do nothing'" (John 15:4-5).

This is a simple concept and yet it conflicts with how Americans think. Being comes before doing. We need to become human beings instead of human doings. To the degree we are being and abiding, to the same degree we will be doing good and bearing fruit. Resting in the Lord, being still, and waiting on God are foreign concepts, and yet they are the biblical model, and they work.

"They who wait for the LORD shall renew their strength; they shall mount up with wings like eagles; they shall run and not be weary; they shall walk and not faint" (Isaiah 40:31). We sing songs about this verse, watch movies with this theme, and often memorize it. But we are crippled when it comes to applying it. We are tired, stressed, and often bear little fruit, but we continue to try harder instead of opening the door and having a quiet cup of tea with Jesus each morning.

I am grateful my foundation crumbled and my world fell apart because God, in His mercy, revealed my faith and trust were not rooted in Christ but on my works. It was not on grace, but on merit. Even though I learned this powerful lesson in 2012, it took two years to sink in. I know the timeline because in 2013, I was a part of a small group studying *Emotionally Healthy Spirituality* by Peter Scazzero (which I highly recommend). We read a chapter each week and then had daily assignments to do each day along with a small amount of time being still.

Each of our daily times waiting on God was to begin with two minutes of stillness. I could not do it. I was unable to just sit quietly in the presence of God. I would rush through the assignment in a few minutes and then go back to work. I feel silly writing this, but it is true.

Recently our small group met again to begin a similar study of another book but decided to review the previous book and see how we were applying the insights we learned last year. As I read through my notes of a year ago, I saw the biggest area of improvement was my ability to be still, rest, and wait. I am now regularly spending a few hours early each morning with my Dad.

I am a quick learner but a slow applier. While I comprehend truth quickly, it takes time before it filters from my head, to my heart, to my hands and feet. It took me a few months to learn to be still. Last summer I was away from home at a small cabin in the mountains. I rode my bike to an overlook and sat and communed with God. I chose the word communed because I did not do all the talking. Some of the time I was still, and other times I asked questions and listened for His response. When I returned, my wife was concerned because I was gone so long. The time flew by as I was in His presence. These were sacred times I am even now reticent to talk about.

Then I began spending the hour before sundown either in my kayak on the lake or walking, which I do even in the winter months. The early morning is nice, but I love the evening. Most of these times of communion and heavenly fellowship occurred while I was not home, where it is too easy to get distracted by emails and daily life. But they also happened when I was outside, with no cell phone and nothing else to occupy my attention. When I am sitting in the middle of a small lake as the golden sun quietly disappears into the horizon, I have nothing to do but draw near to God. Knowing He enjoys these times as much as I do encourages me to seek Him and simply BE, with no agenda or list of requests.

Prayer

Father, by your Spirit, give us a thirst and an appetite for the presence and person of the Living God. Help us work through our own stuff, which keeps us from responding to your invitation to be close to you. Teach us how to be still and commune with you. So be it.

QUESTIONS FOR REFLECTION

1. What is the wonderful way Steve and his son John begin each day? How does this inform and influence Steve's thoughts and actions toward his Heavenly Dad each morning?

2. Luke records a parable Christians call "The Prodigal Son," yet who is the focus of the story? What might be a better title for this parable?

3. Describe the image in Revelation 3:20. Who is being invited? What is God seeking?

4. *"Transformation and change take time and intentionality."* What is your response to this key phrase? How is this principle portrayed in the parable of the sower?

5. Do you have times of being still with God, similar to what Steve describes? If not, do you think it would be possible to try? It might be helpful to discuss with a group, what different ways you can do this in your various walks of life. For example, how can moms with babies and toddlers do this in the midst of sleep deprivation and constant busy-ness?

CHAPTER 12:
LET GOD DEFINE
WHO YOU ARE

The Beloved Son of God

Peter tells us to grow in grace; for it is an ongoing growth process. Perhaps our saturation in the Word is similar to the roots of a tree expanding downward through the rich soil to find nourishment. As the underground foundation is strengthened by its ever expanding infrastructure, the tree is free to grow upwards, the branches broaden outwards, and more fruit is produced. The more we abide in the truth the more fruit we bear.

Jesus was the most grounded person who walked this earth. After devoting training for the good work God uniquely designed for Him, He headed to the Jordan River to be baptized by John. This was a graduation day from His time of preparation. After He emerged from the water, He was given the best presents any graduate could receive: a divine verbal affirmation from His Father and the gift of the Holy Spirit. God affirmed for all the world to hear that this was His beloved boy, and He was well-pleased with Him.

The training period was over, and He was ready to begin His ministry. He had the blessing of His Dad and the presence of the Holy Spirit. He was then led into the wilderness for 40 days to be tempted. At the end of this time of testing, He went from feeling on top of the world to being extremely vulnerable. Not having eaten for 40 days, He was attacked by the devil at the point where He was neediest. When we read this account, we see hunger and bread, but notice the first words out of the liar's mouth: "If you are the Son of God." (Matthew 4:3)

"And when Jesus was baptized, immediately he went up from the water, and behold, the heavens were opened to him, and he saw the Spirit of God descending like a dove and coming to rest on him; and behold, a voice from heaven said, 'This is my beloved Son, with whom I am well pleased.' . . . Then Jesus was led up by the Spirit into the wilderness to be tempted by the devil. And after fasting forty days and forty nights, he was hungry. And the tempter came and said to him, 'If you are the Son of God, command these stones to become loaves of bread.' " (Matthew 3:16-17, 4:1-3).

The devil knew where to attack, the identity of Jesus. I can almost hear him sneer, "If" you are the Son of God. Jesus responded immediately with the word of God and successfully overcame the temptation to doubt who God said He was.

A Beloved Adopted Child of God

Just as it was critical for Jesus to know who He was, it is imperative I know who I am. As our Master was rooted and grounded in the knowledge He was the Son of God, I also need to be assured of who I am in Him. I am not referring to self-confidence, for I have no confidence in the flesh or the natural man.

Neither am I suggesting I accept my unregenerate self as the real me. Rather, I am affirming that when I have been born from above, am in Christ and walking in the Spirit, rooted in the love and truth of God, I am finding my true identity which God intended for me. "For we are his workmanship, created in Christ Jesus for good works, which God prepared beforehand, that we should walk in them" (Ephesians 2:10).

My knowledge of God and His Word informs my heart and mind of my identity. Who I am is based on what He has done and not what I do. God has graciously died for me, redeemed my soul from death, and made me His own adopted child. "To all who did receive him, who believed in his name, he gave the right to become children of God, who were born, not of blood nor of the will of the flesh nor of the will of man, but of God" (John 1:12–13).

I have been born again or born from above and am a new creature in Christ. He saved me by grace, not because of my actions, choices, or good works. What is amazing to me is I seemed to grasp this truth when I first came to Christ because I was fully aware that I had nothing in my hand to bring, except to simply cling to the cross. But then I begin to do better, act better, and accomplish good things for God. In the past two days I have had to battle this very temptation. I have been in a really good place for a long time. Between arising early and investing quality time with God and relating so well to my wife, I thought I was a changed man.

But then I slept in for a few days while I struggled with the beginnings of a sickness, and then while talking with Sandi, my tone was hard and her spirit withered. I was amazed at how quickly I spiraled downward. I felt convicted, condemned, and disappointed. I felt like a failure. God helped me to get back up, make confession, and be restored to Sandi, but I still was under a cloud. Then the Spirit of God communicated to my heart I was still God's son. I won't reveal the specifics as they are personal, but I saw once again how quickly I doubt the truth when I fall.

A few days later Sandi and I discussed this incident. Even though it wasn't pleasant, we faced it, dealt with it, communicated openly, and were restored in a matter of hours. She reminded me, for she is the relationship historian, that had this happened in the past it might have taken weeks before our hearts were together again. I am not saying our life is always peaches and ice cream, but we are learning how to communicate, how to manage our emotions, and how to resolve conflict. These are skills which are essential to becoming a healthy couple. (Speaking the Truth in Love, Lessons I've Learned About Family Communication, was written for couples and families who want to learn how to have safe, open, honest communication. I wrote this book based on what I learned and applied in our own home.)

Who I am is not based on how wonderful I am as a husband or father, or how well I do in business or ministry. It is always based on grace. I am simply growing in grace and appreciating the scope and depth of grace once again today. I wrote this simple illustration in my journal, "An elephant may do things which tempt him to think he is a large cow, but he is still an elephant." I may be tempted to think I am not a child of God, but I am. What I do changes from day to day, but not who I am in the eyes of my God.

I have lived most of my life working and striving to do, so I would have value as a person. The truth is I must first know I am valued before I can effectively do. My lack of a healthy Christ centered self image also made it very difficult to receive input about issues in my life, as I took everything which was said personally. I believe I am making significant progress in this area since I have experienced acceptance and love from Jesus and the body of Christ, for who I am and not for what I have done. I know this will always be an area of weakness but I am encouraged by the changes in my own heart.

It is good to ask ourselves if our self-esteem is tied to something we have accomplished? A mom may define herself by her children. A dad may define himself by his occupation. Or worse yet, parents may define themselves by the accomplishments of their children. Even though raising godly children and working diligently and seeing our children succeed are worthy goals, they must not define who we are. There are numerous illustrations of how we try to impress others by what we do and have done. It is not the doing which is dangerous, but the defining. In our sports crazed society whole cities are depressed when their favorite football team loses, because their personal self-esteem is determined by the success or failure of their team.

There are many other pursuits which can encourage a false sense of who we are. It may be a hobby, a club, fraternity, church, political party, or video game. It may even be really good things, like being a godly husband, or a loving wife, or an anointed evangelist, or a faithful prayer warrior. But these things are what we do and not who we are. I am an adopted child of God, period. I have been saved by grace, period. This is who I am.

If anyone reading this is involved in Christian work, beware of being identified by your ministry. I believe this was a blindspot for me and I resonate with this quote from Dr. Ed Litton who was the senior pastor of the First Baptist Church of Mobile, Alabama. He observed, "Achievement is the opium of this generation of pastor/leaders. Adrenaline is a drug we get addicted to and we see it in the face of our wives before we see it in the mirror, but we'll excuse it as her being ungodly." Dr. Litton lost his wife unexpectedly in 2007 in a car crash and plays the role of Pastor Rogers in the movie Courageous, offering grief counseling to the main character after the loss of his daughter

The Son of God
Jesus was so secure in who He was and in His Father's love He was free to weep at the tomb of

Lazarus, and be laughed at when He was about to raise the dead. He fearlessly spoke the truth to the truth experts of His day. Because He was grounded in the truth of who He was, He was free to be who God designed him to be, stand firm and alone, and be faithful to God's call on His life. He remarked in John 8:29, "He who sent me is with me. He has not left me alone, for I always do the things that are pleasing to him." He lived vertically. His eyes were on God alone.

The Son of Jesse

David was another man secure in who God had made him to be. Even as a youth he stood alone before Goliath, knowing he wasn't really alone, and God had his back. Those lonely years in the wilderness shepherding sheep, guarding them from lions and bears, singing and composing songs, writing in his journal, were his training period when he and God became a team.

Because he was secure in his relationship with the Almighty he was free to be real, honest, and transparent in the Psalms. He was able to dance with abandon before the ark in the streets leading up to Jerusalem. He was able to acknowledge and take full responsibility for his sin with Bathsheba. He became a man after God's heart who walked in his integrity. As I write these words I think it is interesting that what impresses me about David is not his kingdom, or how many battles he won, or how large his armies were, but how real he was. I love David for who he is and not for what he has accomplished.

Psalm 26:11 describes David as walking in his own integrity. "As for me, I shall walk in my integrity; redeem me, and be gracious to me." He was secure in his own identity. He was truthful with himself and others. He knew who he was, and was at peace. David walked in his own integrity. It is a powerful statement I hope we all will be able to say as well. Walking in integrity and being a man of integrity not only benefits the person but his children as well. "The righteous who walks in his integrity—blessed are his children after him!" (Proverbs 20:7).

Our families do not need more money or a bigger house or a fancier vacation, they need Mom and Dad to be fully present, real, vulnerable, and transparent. If parents are not rooted and grounded it is difficult to be open and honest. This was me. I wanted to be real, and I knew it would be a help and encouragement to my sons if I was more transparent and consistent, but I still had so many of my own issues, stuff, failings, shortcomings I was trying to compensate for, I didn't have time for them. I was still trying to grow up to the point I could be a dad. At the time I did not know this, but as I look back, I see I was doing the best I could but avoiding the real work of maturing and developing on the inside.

It was difficult to love my wife as Christ loved me and lay my life down for her when I was still growing up and learning about my own issues. During those early years of beginning our new life together, having children, working, and making plans for the future, I was blissfully occupied and had very little time to reflect or let God search my heart. On the outside I was a young married man with a family, but inside I was the same young boy with all of his baggage. Instead of slowing down and facing my pain, I worked harder, achieved more, and threw myself into worthwhile kingdom-building activities. Because I was not only doing noble things for God but defining myself through my many activities, I postponed the inevitable crash until I was 58. I didn't just experience the loss of my wife, children, business, and ministry in a half hour, I lost myself. I defined myself by how good a husband, father, businessman, and speaker I was.

When I am experiencing grief, the feeling seems to be the reality. I know my situation was not in the same league as Job's loss of everything he held dear, but it still hurt as if it was. When I felt as though I had lost my family, this was acutely painful because I never imagined it would happen. I know I didn't lose them—they were incredibly supportive through the intense few months in 2012—but it felt like it. I identify with Jacob when he saw the blood-stained cloak of many colors and learned Joseph was not coming home. His life unraveled and the hurt was almost unbearable. "All his sons and all his daughters rose up to comfort him, but he refused to be comforted" (Genesis 37:35). I know this feeling.

After my crisis, God began to work deep in my life. Once I knew down in my innermost being God liked me as a person, and He knew me through and through and still loved me, I was able to think of someone else and love them for who they were. I was also able to begin dealing with my own stuff while being transparent and vulnerable with my wife. I now believe before I can love another well, I have to know I am loved myself. The more I am rooted and grounded in Christ alone, the more free I am to be the husband my wife needs.

My vertical relationship with God colors all my horizontal relationships. I cannot emphasize this truth enough. Most of us love as we have been loved. We choose our mate based on our own needs. When we taste divine love and affection and have Christ meet our needs, then we are free to love others.

Our marriage and family have improved as I have become more anchored in the love of God. I also believe the larger body of Christ will grow and prosper when each member of the body is established in the good news of the gospel. When we are free to be who God designed us to be, and not poor imitations of who we think we should be, the whole body can begin to function properly. For the church to benefit, we must each do our own work.

Our Temptation Is Common to Man

The enemy of our souls is the same as the enemy of our Master, and he knows where we are susceptible. When guilt and condemnation are no longer effective, he attacks our identity and who we are in Christ. Shame is the enemy of identity. He whispers, "If you are really a child of God," and just as Jesus responded to the barbs from hell, we need to quote scripture to combat his accusations.

"For all who are led by the Spirit of God are sons of God. For you did not receive the spirit of slavery to fall back into fear, but you have received the Spirit of adoption as sons, by whom we cry, 'Abba! Father!' The Spirit himself bears witness with our spirit that we are children of God, and if children, then heirs—heirs of God and fellow heirs with Christ" (Romans 8:14-17).

God has sent His Spirit to communicate with our spirit we are children of God. We are His kids, His beloved children. No matter how we feel, or what we have done, or how much time we have spent praying or reading the Word, or what kind of spouse or parent we have been today, we belong to Him. He is our Dad. Our Abba Daddy.

The Truth Shall Set You Free

Some mornings I read a page of scripture I refer to as an 'Affirmation'. It is a compilation of passages testifying to who I am in Christ. Jesus was affirmed by His Father. Psalm 139 is an incredible storehouse of truth for every believer. Paul affirmed, "I have been crucified with Christ. It is no longer I who live, but Christ who lives in me." (Galatians 2:20)

Here are several one sentence truths to give you the flavor of what I am assembling. I am still working on this list which has grown to over three pages so far.

I have been created in the image of God.

"God said, 'Let us make man in our image, after our likeness. So God created man in his own image, in the image of God he created him; male and female he created them.'" (Genesis 1:26–27)

I am a temple and habitation of the Holy Spirit.

"Do you not know that you are God's temple and that God's Spirit dwells in you? (1 Corinthians 3:16)

I belong to God.

"You are not your own, for you were bought with a price." (1 Corinthians 6:19–20)

I am an adopted child of God

"Beloved, we are God's children now" (1 John 3:2)

I am forgiven

"I am writing to you, little children, because your sins are forgiven for his name's sake." (1John 2:12)

I am chosen

"He chose us in him before the foundation of the world" (Ephesians 1:4)

I am held and kept

"I give them eternal life, and they will never perish, and no one will snatch them out of my hand." (John 10:28)

I am understood

"For we do not have a high priest who is unable to sympathize with our weaknesses, but one who in every respect has been tempted as we are, yet without sin." (Hebrews 4:15)

If you are interested in receiving a copy of my list email me sdemme@demmelearning.com or go to: http://www.buildingfaithfamilies.org/crisistochrist/

Prayer

Father, Son, and Spirit, enable us to know whose we are, so we will know who we are. Thank you for the witness of the Spirit to confirm our identity as adopted children of God. Deliver us from doubt and let our roots cling to the truths found the inspired words of God. Thank you for being our Dad and making us members of your family. We love and appreciate you.

QUESTIONS FOR REFLECTION

1. What graduation present did Jesus receive? How was this immediately tested?

2. Explain the difference between self-confidence and knowing your identity in Christ. What is your identity in Christ based on?

3. How much your self-esteem tied to something you've accomplished and how much is based on the finished work of Christ? Set aside time for God to search your heart.

4. Give examples of people in the Bible who were secure in who they were, and the subsequent fruit born by this knowledge they possessed.

5. Fill in the blanks and ponder how this truth impacts your own life. "My _____ relationship with God colors all my_____ relationships."

CHAPTER 13: DEEPER ROOTS, BETTER FRUIT

Redeemer and Composter

Now that I am in a better place and have full assurance from the inspired eternal Word of God that I am loved, accepted, adopted, and liked, I can begin to reflect on why I act the way I do and what might be the underlying causes for my behavior. I probably would never have invested time and energy into understanding why I did what I did and reacted the way I had if I had not seen the impact of my behavior on those who were closest to me.

As a husband I can build up my wife, serve her, and love her as Christ loved me and as He loves the church. I can also hurt, wound, crush, and in so many ways, with my words and actions, tear her down. We all are sensitive human beings, but our wives are especially so. They have tender, discerning spirits which sense currents whether spoken or unspoken. This is who they are and how they were designed. If my own stuff is leaking like radioactive waste and wounding my wife, then I need to accept responsibility, play the man, and face it.

In a similar way, as a parent I have tremendous power to influence my children by my walk and my talk. My kids live with me the minute they enter the world. I am the first man they know or observe. My wife and I are the first Christians they meet and watch keenly. Ours is the first marriage they encounter. They learn from us. We have a tremendous responsibility and a wonderful opportunity to impact these young, impressionable lives for eternity. The beauty and the wisdom of the way God created and designed the family is having this power to influence drives us to God to help us be a godly example. We want to be a powerful testimony of the grace and goodness of God.

When I saw the pain my own toxic baggage had caused in my family, I was undone. I was driven to God in a new way. Our family is now in the best place we have ever been, thanks to our God who is the ultimate Redeemer. He works all things for good. But I still need to work with God to face my past, my pain, and my own upbringing in the hopes I can break patterns of behavior and cycles of sin. I heard a speaker recently refer to God as the great Composter, because He takes our manure (a nice word for unpleasant material) and brings good fruit from it. This is the real work, facing our own stuff with God and believing for redemption, healing, and eternal fruit.

Cycle Breaking

My first experience of seeing how my dad had impacted my life had to do with anger. Many years ago my courageous Sandi sat me down and gently told me I had a problem with anger. I knew sometimes I lost my temper, but I did not think it was a big problem. I figured I could master it by being more careful and guarding myself. But after I was angry several more times over the next few months, I realized anger was a serious problem I was unable to fix or control in my own strength. Acknowledging the problem is the beginning of solving it. After six months, I faced the truth I had a problem. I wasn't sure where to turn for help, but remembered James 5:16: "Therefore, confess your sins to one another and pray for one another, that you may be healed."

I was a pastor during this season, and we were soon to have a meeting with fellow leaders of our fellowship. During our time together I confessed my sin to the elders and asked them to pray for me, so I would be healed of anger. I also read a book which had been recommended to me, The Other Side of Love: Handling Anger in a Godly Way by Gary Chapman. Later I listened to a recording of a talk about anger, and attended an anger management conference. Through these various resources, I came to understand some of the causes of anger but was not seeing a significant change in my behavior.

One day in desperation, I knelt by my bed and asked God to deliver me from anger and change my heart. Soon I began to taste more victory, which I now see was grace from God. "God opposes the proud, but gives grace to the humble" (James 4:6). I then confessed my sin to Isaac and three months later to Ethan. I told them I was not a psychologist but wanted to give them an opportunity to tell me about times when I had been angry. I knew if I said

I was genuinely sorry they would quickly forgive me, for they had many times before, but this time I wanted to give them time to think and respond. Their responses were enlightening and freeing.

I was different for some time after facing the problem and seeking to be restored to those I had wounded. I was sharing about this at a conference in Minnesota a few years later and there was a time for questions at the end of the talk. One man asked if my father had had an anger problem. I paused before I answered, and then said, "Yes, he did." I had not thought about this connection before. But as I reflected, I could only recall four or five times when my dad was really angry, but I vividly remember those times and this was over 50 years ago. I wish I could say I saw the benefit of examining my past, hired a therapist, and began to work through other areas which might be hurting those I desperately loved. But I didn't. I thought I was fine and proceeded to live and work hard, as I had always done. But critical mass was finally reached in 2012, and now I am earnestly trying to break cycles in my life so my children don't replicate them in their families. For I am now convinced that just as we receive love and pass it on to those nearest to us, we also pass on pain, unless God helps us to break the cycle.

I have already referenced the pain which Joseph tasted when he was betrayed and abandoned by his family. Seventeen years after Israel and the rest of his family came to Egypt and moved into the land of Goshen, Israel blessed his children and died. Without their father in the picture, Joseph's brothers feared for their lives. They knew Joseph had the power to destroy them and ruin their lives, just as they had sought to ruin his life. But what follows is a wonderful account of a cycle of pain being broken.

"When Joseph's brothers saw that their father was dead, they said, 'It may be that Joseph will hate us and pay us back for all the evil that we did to him.' So they sent a message to Joseph, saying, 'Your father gave this command before he died: "Say to Joseph, 'Please forgive the transgression of your brothers and their sin, because they did evil to you.' "And now, please forgive the transgression of the servants of the God of your father.' Joseph wept when they spoke to him. His brothers also came and fell down before him and said, 'Behold, we are your servants.' But Joseph said to them, 'Do not fear, for am I in the place of God? As for you, you meant evil against me, but God meant it for good, to bring it about that many people should be kept alive, as they are today. So do not fear; I will provide for you and your little ones.' Thus he comforted them and spoke kindly to them" (Genesis 50:15-21).

We know the apple doesn't fall far from the tree. In scripture we are told our sins pass down to a few generations and the blessings of our obedience to a thousand generations. " 'You shall not make for yourself a carved image, or any likeness of anything that is in heaven above, or that is on the earth beneath, or that is in the water under the earth. You shall not bow down to them or serve them; for I the LORD your God am a jealous God, visiting the iniquity of the fathers on the children to the third and fourth generation of those who hate me, but showing steadfast love to thousands of those who love me and keep my commandments' " (Deuteronomy 5:8–10).

There are clear examples of this scripture in the lives of the saints. David was a man after God's own heart, and Jesus was called the Son of David. The blessings of his life impacted the kings of Israel and Judah long after he died. Unfortunately, the sins associated with his adulterous affair with Bathsheba and his murder of Uriah were felt in his own home. Absalom sought to usurp the throne and murder his father. Parents do impact the lives of their children.

Let me encourage you to take some time and hearken back to what your parents were like. You can either do this by yourself or with your spouse, and perhaps even with your children. I have done this exercise more than once and continue to make notes about my folks, who have both passed on. I wish I could sit down and ask them so many questions, but all I have now are my memories and the recollections of others who knew them well. I think you will be surprised at the impact this assignment will have on you.

I used to mistakenly think I was my own man, an individual. I see now how many of my values were absorbed from my family and how much I am like my father and mother. Ethan often introduces me to his colleagues by saying the tree doesn't grow far from the apple. This is a true observation and always brings a smile to both of us. We are each our parents' children and bear their imprint.

I had some areas in which I was upset at my folks for the way they raised me. But after looking at their lives and the challenges they faced growing up in their own families (my grandparents), I was left with a profound sense of gratitude for how well they did considering the circumstances of their childhoods. I felt only compassion and forgiveness instead of bitterness and anger over what they lacked. You may feel differently when you are done, but either way, facing these truths will improve your own parenting. For you can't break cycles until you identity them.

The Past

"One learns of the pain of others by suffering one's own pain, by turning inside oneself, by finding one's own soul. And it is important to know of pain. It destroys our self-pride, our arrogance, and our indifference toward others. It makes us aware of how frail and tiny we are and of how much we must depend upon the Master of the Universe." Chaim Potok, The Chosen.

I can't change my past. As a Christian I know God works (has worked, is working, and will work) ALL THINGS together "for good." (Romans 8:28) Knowing that God is sovereign and that He has my back helps me to trust Him and gives me hope. Someone has said, "Every saint has a past, and every sinner has a future." While I don't see the whole picture, I do recognize the past has shaped me and made me who I am. I may have done things for which I am rightly ashamed, but this doesn't change who I am. Because of Jesus, I am an adopted child of God, loved, accepted, and liked. May God help me to face what has gone before, own it, and make peace with it, without letting it define me.

I am currently reading Genesis again, as it is the start of a new year. I have thought about how God used the painful experiences of life in Potiphar's house and in prison to prepare Joseph for being the new prime minister. He obviously learned the language, had time to understand the political climate, and by spending time with the chief butler and baker, got a glimpse into the character and personality of Pharaoh. When he emerged from the dungeon he was ready to govern.

When I was an assistant to the pastor of a small church I was encouraged to find work in the community. I was first hired by a cabinet shop. Listening to loud, raucous sounds (they called it rock music) all day was difficult, as was breathing sawdust and lacquer fumes. But I made a lifelong friend there who became like a brother, acquired skills I have used repeatedly as a home owner, and learned what life was like in the construction industry.

After this job, I was hired as a substitute teacher in the local high school, which turned into a full-time job two weeks later. With no education classes from college and without a full major in math, I became a math instructor. For the next few years I took classes at night at a local university and taught 15-18-year-olds. I felt I was not following my calling as a minster of the gospel, but God knew my future.

A few years later, when I was in the ministry full time, our youngest child was born with Down Syndrome, which led to an emotional and physical breakdown for my wife and myself after his many trips to the hospital. I resigned from all of my commitments, felt like a failure, moved out of state, and began tutoring in math to put bread on the table. This led to writing Math-U-See, speaking at conferences, writing books for Building Faith Families. This is my past. I did not understand it when I was in it, but without it, I would not be who I am or where I am. God is good, all the time.

Issues

I was misunderstood as a youth. I have experienced rejection from close friends, including people I admired and looked up to as Christian mentors. David understood the feeling. Consider this excerpt from his journal: "My heart throbs; my strength fails me, and the light of my eyes—it also has gone from me. My friends and companions stand aloof from my plague, and my nearest kin stand far off" (Psalm 38:10-11). David suffered being estranged from his companions and his family.

I have also been falsely accused by others in the church. Those were hard experiences, especially since the false accusations came from those I loved and respected and from whom I expected better. Once again, the words of David were a help to me. "For it is not an enemy who taunts me—then I could bear it; it is not an adversary who deals insolently with me—then I could hide from him. But it is you, a man, my equal, my companion, my familiar friend. We used to take sweet counsel together; within God's house we walked in the throng" (Psalm 55:12–14).

When we follow Christ for any significant length of time, we will experience misunderstanding, rejection, and false accusations. Unfortunately, these sad occurrences are normal as long as we are with other people. I am also learning until I make peace with these experiences and learn to accept them, they will fester and become toxic waste to those closest to me, especially my wife and family. "If one member suffers, all suffer together; if one member is honored, all rejoice together" (1 Corinthians 12:26). A family is a mini body of Christ, and when one person hurts, all hurt to some degree. We all share in each other's sufferings as well as in times of rejoicing.

But it has been a revelation to discover ultimately the problem is not the people in the church, or my family, or my close Christian friends; it is within my own heart. I have been helped by this quote, of unknown source: "Healing doesn't mean the damage never existed. It means the damage no longer controls our lives." When I am not in a good place, I tend to blame others and be critical of their actions and behaviors. My poor wife has had to listen to me rant when I was hurt by others. I did not respond in the Spirit, I reacted in the flesh. When I was offended, somebody else was to blame. I didn't have the maturity to act like a Christian. I was not rooted and grounded in God's acceptance but in how I was accepted by others, which is a fragile place to be.

The more I am able to know and taste the unconditional mercy of God the more I can move on to let the past go, forgive the offender, and move on to loving him. Another quote by an unknown author captures this truth: "I don't know the actual meaning of maturity, but for me, maturity is when a person hurts you, and you try to understand their situation rather than hurting them back."

David and Jonathan were blameless young men, but Saul was haunted and hounded by his own personal insecurities and demons. Several times he tried to not only kill David but threw a spear at his own son. "Saul sought to pin David to the wall with the spear, but he eluded Saul, so that he struck the spear into the wall. And David fled and escaped that night" (1 Samuel 19:10). "But Saul hurled his spear at him [Jonathan] to strike him. So Jonathan knew that his father was determined to put David to death" (1 Samuel 20:33). They did not do anything wrong, but they were recipients of the toxicity within his own breast. He was projecting his personal issues on those who loved him best and were closest to him.

I have often thought of the admonition to fathers to not provoke your children or discourage them. Certainly Saul provoked Jonathan and discouraged him. May God help us fathers to acknowledge our pain and play the man in coming to grips with our toxic stuff, so we don't exasperate our children and cause them to lose heart.

"Fathers, do not provoke your children to anger" (Ephesians 6:4).

"Fathers, do not provoke your children, lest they become discouraged." (Colossians 3:21)

"Fathers, do not exasperate your children, so that they will not lose heart." (Colossians 3:21 NASB)

In the past two years I have sat down with my three older sons, all sterling young men, and told them I was willing to listen to anything they had to get off their chest from issues they have with me. I told them I knew they had forgiven me, but I also knew I had hurt and wounded them many times, and I wanted them to be whole, experience healing, and have closure. If this meant meeting with them by themselves, or with their wives or a counselor, I was willing.

Over the past year I have had several sessions with one son. Over the course of several months he would mention something from the past which would trigger one of my buttons. I knew he was testing me to see how I would respond. This is similar to poking a snake with a stick to ensure it is really dead. Finally we made an appointment to talk. This was two years later in 2014.

During this three-hour meeting, where many tears were shed, I learned why he was so in tune with me. We used to joke I could just look at something and he would know what I was thinking. What I didn't know was this was because whenever I was in the room he would focus his spiritual antenna to sense my moods so he could be prepared if I started slinging spears around the room. I know now, as never before, it only takes a harsh word, or a look, or a sarcastic comment to wound my family. I was their dad whom they loved. I could build them up or I could wound them.

Where did my own hurts emanate from? Now I am in a good place with God, I am willing to explore my past. I have come to the conclusion there were two significant factors which contributed to my crisis. I didn't fully understand the gospel, and I had been hurt growing up in my own family.

Learning about the good news, I now know I am already pleasing to God, because of the gift of forgiveness and the gift of righteousness through Jesus. This conviction lets me rest in the Lord, instead of always striving to do more for God. Always working, pushing, striving left me with very little gasoline in my own tank for the relationships which matter most. I was giving life my best shot but was spread too thin. Are you overextended? Are you being led, or driven? Is the yoke and burden you are carrying from God or from yourself? Jesus says in Matthew 11:28-30, "Come to me, all who labor and are heavy laden, and I will give you rest.

Take my yoke upon you, and learn from me, for I am gentle and lowly in heart, and you will find rest for your souls. For my yoke is easy, and my burden is light." The burden I was bearing was exhausting and I was on the edge of burnout regularly, especially in the spring (which I learned from my observant son).

God gives rest for the weary, peace for the troubled(John 14:27), and water for the thirsty(John 5:37). When the disciples came to report to Jesus all they had done, He directed them to take some time and rest. "The apostles returned to Jesus and told him all that they had done and taught. And he said to them, "Come away by yourselves to a desolate place and rest a while." For many were coming and going, and they had no leisure even to eat." (Mark 6:30-31) Taking time to rest is still hard for me, but I am learning.

I want to write this next paragraph in an honoring spirit. I love my dad and mom, but we had our struggles. As much as I loved, admired, and respected my dad, we did not have a close relationship. As I studied his life, I realized he was a much nicer guy than his dad, and I honor him for this. But we still were not close. I admired my mom and we were a lot alike, but I never felt like I could please her. The last time she visited us, we spent days taking her and her sister on day trips and rolling out the red carpet. On the way to the airport for their return flight, she told me what we had not done the week she was here. Apparently one of them had a bucket list of sorts and we had not done what they were hoping to do. It would have been nice to know of the list seven days sooner, but alas, 'twas too late now. Now I could write a book of happy memories of these two precious people I am glad and thankful to call Mom and Dad, but there were issues, and if you have read this far you can see how these earthly connections impacted my view of God. My heavenly Father and I were not tight, and I thought I could never please Him. Suffice to say, my relationship with my parents had a huge impact on me.

I cannot change my past. I cannot choose my parents, or my siblings. But these family relationships played a huge role in my development, shaped me, and made me who I am today. I can choose whether I will let these things have power over me. I am convinced until I face the past and make peace with it, the wounds and hurts will continue to make themselves felt in the present and influence the way I live and relate to my own family.

My Stuff

I realize it may sound like I am blaming my lack of understanding of the gospel and my parents for my issues. I don't want to give this impression for it is not true. They are significant factors, but there is another big obstacle: me. I have plenty of my own issues that were independent of theology or parenting, mainly my own pride. If I had an ear to hear and been able to hear the quiet input from my wife, or observed the signals from my kids, or been open to input from others, I could have headed this crisis off much sooner. But I didn't want to ask for help. I especially didn't want to appear like a loser asking a therapist for counsel. I reasoned I could fix this myself, I just needed to work harder. It grieves me to think how much stress and pain I have brought on those closest to me by being afraid to humble myself and seek help. Sure I had a hard year, but my wife and children had tough decades with the very person who was authorized to nurture, love, and protect them.

Brennan Manning puts it this way, "To live by grace means to acknowledge my whole life story, the light side and the dark. In admitting my shadow side I learn who I am and what God's grace means." The result is my mess has become my message. The worst day in my life, when I felt like I had lost all, led me through a painful journey where I encountered Jesus and learned He liked me. Now I am in the best place I have ever been with those who mean the most to me, God and my family.

Prayer

God help us acknowledge our past, the good, the bad, and the ugly. Teach us to cast our burdens into your lap and allow them to work for our good and the good of others. Walk through the dark chapters in our life and redeem them for your glory. "If I say, 'Surely the darkness shall cover me, and the light about me be night,' even the darkness is not dark to you; the night is bright as the day, for darkness is as light with you." (Psalm 139:11–12)

QUESTIONS FOR REFLECTION

1. How is God the great Composter? What is the "real work" for us?

2. *"I am now convinced that just as we receive love and pass it on to those nearest us, we also pass on pain, unless God helps us to break the cycle."* Steve faced his anger, confessed it, and asked God for deliverance. At one point he remembered his own dad also had anger issues. What are some things you struggle with that you can't seem to change? Take time to reflect what your parents were like. Identify cycles in your family. Pray for compassion and grace to acknowledge and forgive your parents' shortcomings.

3. Respond to this quote by Chaim Potok: *"One learns of the pain of others by suffering one's own pain, by turning inside oneself, by finding one's own soul. And it is important to know of pain. It destroys our self-pride, our arrogance, and our indifference toward others. It makes us aware of how frail and tiny we are and of how much we must depend upon the Master of the Universe."*

4. Steve lists some difficult life experiences which yielded helpful results years later. Do you have any similar experiences in which hindsight reveals the way God was working all things together for good?

5. Have you experienced misunderstanding, rejection, and/or false accusations? Have you learned to accept them? Remember: "Healing doesn't mean the damage never existed. It means the damage no longer controls our lives."

CHAPTER 14:
SEARCH ME O GOD

Baggage and the Two Biggies

There are two commandments which are paramount, to love God with everything in us and to love others as we have been loved. Loving God is called by Jesus the "great and first commandment." (Matthew 22:38). Then in John 13 and 15, He articulates what He calls the New Commandment, "A new commandment I give to you, that you love one another: just as I have loved you" (John 13:34).

I know from countless hours in scripture that God is love. I am convinced He loves and likes me. John informs me that my ability to love God and others is a result of God taking the initiative and loving me first (1 John 4:19). SO I ask myself, what keeps me from apprehending this clear message? I have concluded the signal from heaven is being broadcast clearly but my antenna is faulty. My stuff, and my baggage, are corrupting my ability to download the message.

I am willing to have God search me and reveal my stuff it will help me love Him more and love others as I have been loved. I met with a therapist in 2012 because I was desperate. I have been seeing a new therapist for the past two years, because, as Shrek reminds us, ogres have layers! If my wounds and scars from my past are contributing to not see God clearly nor comprehend His love, I can either confront my baggage with God's help, or watch my own stuff hinder my ability to love well.

Search My Heart

Jews in the first century wanted a powerful Messiah to deliver them from the oppression of Rome. Jesus looked beyond what they wanted and provided what they needed, inner healing from sin and its effects. He worked in their hearts. He didn't send an army; He sent the Holy Spirit.

"It is my experience after 40 years as a priest that we could say the same about many well-intentioned Christians and clergy. Their religion has never touched them or healed them at the unconscious level where all of the real motivation, hurts, unforgiveness, anger, wounds, and illusions are stored, hiding—and often fully operative." *Breathing Under Water* by Richard Rohr.

This is new territory for me. I have not been given to stopping, resting, being still, or asking God to search my heart like David. "Search me, O God, and know my heart! Try me and know my thoughts!" (Psalm 139:23) I can recall one experience which occurred when I was in seminary and had just returned from a weekend retreat. It was obvious to all who attended the retreat God had met us and worked deeply in many people's hearts. The messages were anointed, as was the worship. Everyone seemed moved, except me. I was puzzled.

I came home and began thinking about whether I had an unconfessed sin, or somewhere I had strayed, which would cut me off from the obvious blessing of the presence of God. But I couldn't come up with anything. Not knowing where to turn, I made an appointment to seek counsel from a godly professor.

As I described my condition, he suggested I read a sermon by Charles Finney entitled "Breaking Up the Fallow Ground." The primary thought I recalled from the sermon was comparing our hearts to hard, unplowed, fallow ground, which is like a field in the early spring, before the farmer plowed the land in preparation for planting the seeds. As I read, I was convicted that I had a hard heart.

Somehow I knew what I had to do but was not excited at the prospect. Saturday morning came around. I did all the mundane chores I could think of, then closed the door to my room, knelt by my bed, and asked God to show me my sin and soften my heart. I got a glimpse of my own condition and wept for a season. When I arose, I was a repentant, soft-hearted Christian. It was painful, but helpful, because I did not like living with a hardened heart.

About this same time I found one of my favorite scriptures, "I will sprinkle clean water on you, and you shall be clean from all your uncleannesses, and from all your idols I will cleanse you. And I will give you a new heart, and a new spirit I will put within you. And I will remove the heart of stone from your flesh and give you a heart of flesh. And I will put my Spirit within you, and cause you to walk in my statutes and be careful to obey my rules." (Ezekiel 36:25-27) For many weeks I began each day asking God to take out anything stony in my heart and replace it with a soft heart of flesh, and He did. I still ask God for a soft heart regularly.

Examine Yourselves

2 Corinthians 13:5 tells us, "Examine yourselves," and believers are encouraged to examine themselves before partaking of the Lord's Supper. "Let a person examine himself, then, and so eat of the bread and drink of the cup" (1 Corinthians 11:28). David went further and asked God to examine him: "Examine me, O LORD, and try me; test my mind and my heart" (Psalm 26:2). Hebrews 4:12 shows us the Word of God can enable us to discern the condition of our heart. "For the word of God is living and active, sharper than any two-edged sword, piercing to the division of soul and of spirit, of joints and of marrow, and discerning the thoughts and intentions of the heart."

Looking back over my life as a believer, I see I am usually quick to respond to conviction of sin from the Spirit of God, for I do not enjoy being separated from God because of sin. But it has been a revelation to me to recognize how important in the sight of God are relationships between people. Jesus said there are only two commands: love God and love others. As I have attempted to point out, I have learned the hard way how my relationship with God determines how well I relate to my family and others. Notice how loving God and others are interrelated in 1 John 4:19-20, "We love because he first loved us. If anyone says, 'I love God,' and hates his brother, he is a liar; for he who does not love his brother whom he has seen cannot love God whom he has not seen."

So how do I discern whether I am loving others well? How do I examine myself in light of the two great commands? Here are some lessons I have learned which I hope you will find helpful.

Specks and Logs

"Why do you see the speck that is in your brother's eye, but do not notice the log that is in your own eye? Or how can you say to your brother, 'Let me take the speck out of your eye,' when there is the log in your own eye? You hypocrite, first take the log out of your own eye, and then you will see clearly to take the speck out of your brother's eye" (Matthew 7:3-5). Specks which aggravate us in someone else's eye reveal the log in our own eye. There is a wonderful word, "blindspot," which we generally use in reference to driving a car. A blindspot is something we cannot see. The application here is we cannot see ourselves. Jesus teaches us to examine ourselves by taking note of what we are offended by in others. The question is, what bugs us about other people? This insignificant issue they have may turn out to be a significant log in our own life.

Let me give one humorous example and one convicting one. When my wife and I visit someone's home which is full of clutter we generally come home and clean our own house. Instead of laughing and making critical comments about their housekeeping, we try to take care of our own house.

Now the convicting one, as described by C. S. Lewis in **Mere Christianity**: "Today I come to that part of Christian morals where they differ most sharply from all other morals. There is one vice of which no man in the world is free; which everyone loathes when he sees it in someone else; and of which hardly any people, except Christians, ever imagine that they are guilty themselves. I have heard people admit that they are bad-tempered, or that they cannot keep their heads about girls or drink, or even that they are cowards. I do not think I have ever heard anyone who was not a Christian accuse himself of this vice. And at the same time I have very seldom met anyone, who was not a Christian, who showed the slightest mercy to it in others. There is no fault that makes a man more unpopular, and no fault which we are more unconscious of in ourselves. And the more we have it ourselves, the more we dislike it in others. The vice I am talking of is Pride or Self-Conceit: and the virtue opposite to it, in Christian morals, is called Humility."

The one phrase which strikes me is "the more we have it ourselves, the more we dislike it in others." May God help me to see my blindspots by what I see in someone else.

Buttons

When the boys were younger we used to notice when they were mad at one another, they reacted by pushing each other's buttons. I don't remember the exact situation, but I commented to Isaac on one occasion, "You sure know how to push Joseph's buttons," to which he replied, "His whole body is a button." Today they are the best of friends. But it seems no one knows the hotspots of another like a sibling. If I really want to identify my own buttons, I may consider asking those closest to me if they notice when and what sets me off. This takes a great degree of humility and teachability. When I do ask for help I have to remember the person I am asking also pays a price and has a risk in being truthful.

What if I ask for insight from them and then react emotionally when I hear their input. What if I get upset and reject what they say? How will I respond? Will I get angry? Will I be sarcastic and later throw it back in their face? Am I safe? is the big question. If I have a history of anger and intimidation it will take time and practice to rebuild trust and confidence so my intimate friends and family feel safe revealing my needs. It is hard to ask, but it is hard to answer as well. If my friends and family do give me wise counsel, I hope I will have grace to thank them and then reflect on what they said and go to my knees. I don't want to shoot the messenger and miss the message.

Trap Doors and Triggers

I took a class on family therapy last fall and learned about something called an introject or trigger. This is a term used to describe an emotional trap door associated with an historic event. For example, if someone was constantly criticized as a child, whether by a parent, sibling, or teacher, they will feel inadequate. They may grow up to be a successful entrepreneur but if someone criticizes them, they will still battle feelings of inadequacy regardless of how old they are or how many businesses they have started.

These events which happened in our childhood are still present in who we are today. Perhaps you did not receive unconditional love as a child but were rejected by one or both of your parents. You will feel rejected. Even when you become a mature, accomplished adult, if you face rejection, you will feel unworthy and unloved.

The good news is when we learn to identify these triggers and the historical event to which they are attached, we can develop strategies to rob them of their power. We all have these triggers and trap doors. And they are always present. They are common to man.

One significant issue I have from my childhood was not having a father in my life throughout the week. He was only home on weekends and holidays. I went through therapy and identified this lack of the presence of my dad, impacted me more than I knew. To this day I have a deep-rooted fear of being abandoned, especially by those whom I expect to be there for me. Understanding what my family was like in my early formative years gave me new information which has helped me work through feeling abandoned now.

One December I had a chance to apply what I had been learning about my own emotional trap door of feeling abandoned. My wife had been making plans to go up to a cabin in the mountains for a weekend with a few of her close girlfriends and was quite excited at the prospect. John and I would be bachelors while they were gone, but I was okay with the prospect. Sandi and I had talked about it several weeks before and I had encouraged her to go and have a great time. She derives as much pleasure from anticipating and planning an event as the event itself (unlike me). She cheerfully made her preparations for some time leading up to the weekend.

Then another friend, whom she hadn't seen in years, called and said she was coming through the following weekend. Sandi really wanted to take her to the mountains as well, and I said sure, have another lovely time. And for the next few days all I heard were pieces of conversations on the phone with her friends about these two upcoming weekends. Sandi was bubbling and happy about the prospects of entertaining some of her favorite people at one of her favorite places. And Steve was beginning to feel hurt and abandoned.

I recognized what was happening, and instead of denying the hurt, emotionally shutting down, and withdrawing into my cave, I asked Sandi if we could talk. We sat down and I shared how I was feeling. While I wanted her to have a good time, I was feeling left out, sad, and alone. She was completely empathetic and thanked me for talking about what I was experiencing. Then the pain left and I was okay. Bringing my introject to the light, discussing it openly, and acknowledging my hurt, had robbed it of its power.

I fully expect to continue to be vulnerable to pain from my past and perhaps identify other introjects, and I know as I confront and embrace them they will have less and less power.

Anger

Anger can be an emotion, but it can also be a defense mechanism to guard me from being known, exposed, and vulnerable. I can hide behind it and lose myself in it. Generally I try to avoid shame and nakedness at any cost, even to the point of attacking, wounding, intimidating, controlling, and shutting out those closest to me who only have my best interests at heart. Much like Saul with David and Jonathan, Saul was angry, but his issues were in his own heart. When I am angry I put distance between myself and others.

Anger, while destructive to those receiving the brunt of it, can also be an incredible learning tool. When I have cooled down, I ask myself, and God, Why was I angry? What pushed my button? What offended me?

Within

As we have seen, the battle we each face as we arise each morning is within our own hearts. I have heard it said of St. Francis, who upon beginning the day, would address his carnal self, "Good morning, Brother Ass." James 4:1 states, "What causes quarrels and what causes fights among you? Is it not this, that your passions are at war within you?" This is a biblical concept. If we are struggling with improper speech, we do not seek to curb our tongue, we examine our heart, for "out of the abundance of the heart the mouth speaks" (Matthew 12:34). We do not have a tongue issue but a heart issue. There is much more to say about the war in our members between the flesh and the Spirit but I will address this later in the book. For now I want to tell you how God has led me to begin each day to help with this battle with my own "Brother Steve."

"When I was young I set out to change the world. When I grew a little older, I perceived this was too ambitious, so I set out to change my state. This too I realized was too ambitious, so I set out to change my own town. When I realized I could not even do this, I tried to change my family. Now as an old man I know I should have started by changing myself. If I had started by changing myself, maybe then I would have succeeded in changing my family, the town, and even the state, and who knows maybe even the world." Hasidic rabbi on his deathbed, quoted in *Emotionally Healthy Spirituality* by Peter Scazzero.

Prayer

"Search me, O God, and know my heart! Try me and know my thoughts! And see if there be any grievous way (or way of pain) in me, and lead me in the way everlasting!" (Psalms 139:23–24)

QUESTIONS FOR REFLECTION

1. Take some time to have God search your heart. What is its condition? Is it a heart of stone or a heart of flesh? Pray Ezekiel 36:25–27, inserting your own name.

2. Summarize the application of Jesus' instruction about specks and logs in Matthew 7:3–5. Do you have any true life experiences illustrating this which you can share?

3. What does Steve say to do if you want to identify your own "buttons"? How can you apply this technique?

4. Define an introject and give an example. Think about your own emotional trap doors. Write about one or more that come to your mind. See if you can brainstorm and develop some strategies to rob the introject of its power.

5. How can emotions such as anger be defense mechanisms? In contrast, how can your emotions be a gift to you?

CHAPTER 15:
ABIDING

My Good Place with Dad

My goal each day is to get my heart, soul, mind, and spirit in a place of peace and rest. I want to be at peace with God and at peace in myself. This is a daily discipline. I have found I cannot take a day off or coast on the previous day. We each have to work out our own salvation, but for me, how I begin the day is critical to how I am throughout the day. A few minutes every day, becoming more rooted in the word and God's love makes all the difference. What I currently do begins the night before, when I go to bed at a reasonable time. "It is in vain that you rise up early and go late to rest, eating the bread of anxious toil; for he gives to his beloved sleep" (Psalm 127:2). God has made me what time I need to get up and begin my day with Him. The past several months of following this regimen has borne really good, consistent fruit.

I rarely wake up in a state of peace, but I work with God until I am. "Let us therefore strive to enter that rest" (Hebrews 4:11). I do not fully understand what the writer of Hebrews is talking about when he mentions the place of rest. But I do think about the phrase "strive to enter" because it takes effort on my part each day. I desire to be in perfect peace, because when I am at peace on the inside, I can be kind, patient, and gentle on the outside. The battle is not outside, but inside. It is not people or circumstances but my own heart. A scripture which has helped me in this struggle is Isaiah 26:3: "You keep him in perfect peace whose mind is stayed on you, because he trusts in you."

I am attempting to put God foremost in my thoughts, to keep my mind focused, or as another version puts it, "whose thoughts are fixed on you" (NLT). I am consciously redirecting my thoughts Godward. I am finding peace in this activity. I am also seeking to trust in God. I need to be reminded often God is indeed sovereign and rules in the affairs of men. There is no quicker way to stop being at peace than to watch the evening news, read the newspaper, and fill your mind with events which seem out of control and disheartening. The antidote is to fix our thoughts on God and trust in His sovereign control over all the affairs of men. I recently assembled a list of scriptures on this topic to read when I struggle with trusting God. When God is at the forefront of my mind and I am trusting Him, I am at peace.

"Yours, O LORD, is the greatness and the power and the glory and the victory and the majesty, for all that is in the heavens and in the earth is yours. Yours is the kingdom, O LORD, and you are exalted as head above all. Both riches and honor come from you, and you rule over all. In your hand are power and might, and in your hand it is to make great and to give strength to all" (1 Chronicles 29:11–12).

Most days I begin by being still, then read a structured set of scriptures I have pulled together, followed by prayer and being still. Some days I begin my time with God by listening to uplifting music. I prefer to sing along with the music if I can (without waking my family) as this engages my mind and enhances the worship experience. This is a new territory for me as I used to arise, plow through my bible reading, go through my prayer list, then attack the day. I rarely was able to stop and be still and give heed to my spirit. I spent a few minutes "doing my devotions" but rarely invested time to connect with God or listen to His still, small voice. This new life I am experiencing requires new spiritual disciplines, and takes effort. But it is good work and bears good fruit in my relationship with God and others.

Etymologists speculate the expression "good-bye" is derived from the longer phrase "May God be with ye." Similarly, "good morning" may come from "May God give you a good morning" or a "good day." How I begin each morning sets the tone for the rest of the day. When I want to have a "God" day or a "good" day, then I begin the day by meeting God and investing time in His presence.

I still battle with believing the gospel, but I am fully convinced the battle is in my own head. For I am persuaded God likes me, I just have trouble receiving the message. The message being broadcast from heaven is "I love you, you are mine." But my spiritual antenna has to be adjusted each day to pick up the clear signal.

I know when I draw near to God, He draws near to me. As I meditate on the truth, I recall scriptures which inform my mind of the veracity of His love and the unchangeableness of His nature.

For several weeks, my prayer when I awake has been Psalm 90:14: "Satisfy me in the morning with your steadfast love, that I may rejoice and be glad all my days." I love this scripture. The writer of this prayer may have been tempted to doubt God's love, but asked God to help him. (The original text reads, "Satisfy us in the morning with your steadfast love, that we may rejoice and be glad all our days." I often personalize the scripture by changing the plural pronouns "us" and "we" to the singular "I" and "me.")

Here are some other scriptures which encourage me in the morning:

- "Let me hear in the morning of your steadfast love, for in you I trust" (Psalm 143:8).
- "The steadfast love of the LORD never ceases; his mercies never come to an end; they are new every morning; great is your faithfulness" (Lamentations 3:22-23).
- "How precious to me are your thoughts, O God! How vast is the sum of them! If I would count them, they are more than the sand. I awake, and I am still with you" (Psalms 139:17-18).

Recognizing my natural proclivity to think God is emotionally distant, I devote time to read and meditate on a biblical picture of God, whose thoughts toward me are precious and more than the sand. I also remind myself of the character and nature of God. He is faithful, and his steadfast love never ceases.

One of my favorite verses is John 15:9: "As the Father has loved me, so have I loved you." This scripture was used by the Holy Spirit to convince my heart and my mind how much Jesus loved and liked me. It ends with these challenging four words: "Abide in My love." Those words exhort me to not only taste of the love of God, but abide, live, and pitch my tent on this truth and stay there. I have a tendency to experience truth but then gradually resort to my default settings. But those words have made me know God wants me to move to a new level of understanding of this critical fact, He loves and likes me, and remain there. The Greek root of abide is meno, from which we get the word "remain."

To this end I deliberately invest time to study the grace and care of God for me. In my study I have compiled over 40 lists of scriptures, which I call "Meditations" and which I frequently marinate in my time alone with God. I am happy to share these studies with you on my website, www. buildingfaithfamilies.org. If you can't find them, email me sdemme@demmelearning.com.

Gospel Centered

In hindsight, I recognize by not understanding the completeness of the gospel of grace, and being rooted and grounded in God's love, contributed greatly to my crisis in 2012. Comprehending grace and the good news more fully and being rooted and grounded in the knowledge that God knows me, loves me, and likes me has led to my restoration.

Over the past several years I have addressed thousands of earnest believers and have discovered many of them do not believe, in their innermost heart, that God loves them, likes them, and is pleased with them. As a result we are crippled in our ability to give and receive love, which is the heart of the matter. I have lived in a state of semi-condemnation for years and do not plan on returning. Instead I have moved my tent and am diligently working to abide in His love.

I have written another book, *Knowing God's Love*, which goes into more detail on abiding and being rooted and grounded in love and grace.

Prayer

"May the Lord direct your hearts to the love of God and to the steadfastness of Christ." (2 Thessalonians 3:5)

QUESTIONS FOR REFLECTION

1. Describe the daily discipline Steve discusses at the beginning of this chapter, which has been fruitful for him.

2. What is the antidote to feeling stressed and discouraged about the news when you hear or see it on TV or the newspaper or online? How can you be at peace?

3. Summarize the way Steve used to begin his day and how he begins it now. Circle the differences.

4. Consider posting 1 Chronicles 29:11–12 and Psalm 90:14 somewhere where you can see them as you begin your morning routine. Personalize them.

5. How do we avoid our tendency to experience truth but then gradually revert back to our default settings?

CHAPTER 16: LIVING IN GRACE

Earthen Vessels

The past four years have been a time of upheaval, pain, blessing, crisis, and learning. God has been teaching and transforming me from the inside out. But change takes time and requires patience and forgiveness— for myself. There will be wonderful weeks where I am in a good place and Sandi and I are communicating well and connected in new and special ways. Then something will happen (called life), and it will seem like I am back to square one again, only I'm not.

Even when the discordant notes enter my life, I find I have new tools to manage my emotions and find my way back to God. When Sandi and I have a small conflict of some sort, we have learned (and are always learning) how to identify what is happening, communicate, and deal with it in a matter of hours. In the past, these kind of tiffs might have lingered for days or weeks before we were in harmony again. In other words, we are still human and still have our own baggage, but in our journey together we are so much better equipped to address the situations as they arise and face them side by side.

God says we have this treasure in earthen vessels or jars of clay. Or I like to translate this verse, we are each cracked pots. The whole verse reads, "We have this treasure in jars of clay, to show that the surpassing power belongs to God and not to us"

(2 Corinthians 4:7). I think of myself as a cracked pot, but God is more generous. Consider what He says in Psalm 103:13-14, "As a father shows compassion to his children, so the LORD shows compassion to those who fear him. For he knows our frame; he remembers that we are dust." He knows I am human. Even though I have been created in His image, I also need to rest, take naps, eat regularly, and find His easy yoke and His light burden. I depend on God more than I ever have. I am learning to be content, knowing I am still learning and growing. Life is a journey and growth is a process, and I am simply pressing on, while abiding.

Sandi and I are learning to accept each other for who we are, and where we are on this pilgrimage. Sometimes the hard part for me is to forgive myself when I slip back into my own stuff and tend to be hard on myself. But I know if God has forgiven Steve, I should be able to forgive Steve. Everything about the gospel applies to me as well as to others. God likes me whether I have good quiet times in the morning or not. He loves me perfectly, knowing everything about me. His love covers a multitude of sins. There is no condemnation, nor shame, nor accusation from the pit, which has any power over God's children. Even if my own heart condemns me, God is greater than my heart. This I recall to mind, therefore I have hope, I remember I am a cracked pot. Thankfully God chooses and likes cracked pots, because He is a God of grace.

As you read the Bible, notice all the imperfect people in it. Remember the disciples quarreling and squabbling, before and after Pentecost. Besides debating who would be the greatest in the kingdom, recall Peter being confronted by Paul in Galatia. Those men were human. We are human. In fact, the shortest list you will ever make is of the perfect families in scripture, for there aren't any. This doesn't mean we quit growing, but let the world, the flesh, and the devil be your only enemies and don't help them by beating yourself up. This is the job of our enemy, the accuser of the brethren.

I do want to encourage those of you who have read thus far that being rooted and grounded and in a good place with God pays big dividends and bears good fruit in my marriage and in my family. We are learning how to communicate, openly and honestly. Sandi and I set aside time each week to have what we call "chair chats." Sometimes we have issues to address, but most of the time we just communicate and make sure we are good together. One morning, Sandi had a specific topic she wanted to tell me. She began by saying that what she had to say would be hard for me to hear, but it had worked out okay. Then as she talked I listened, I mean really listened. I gave her my undivided attention, looked in her eyes, and was totally present. When she was done, I was quiet and a few tears had welled up in my eyes. I said, "That must have been really hard, I am so sorry." Then in amazement, she responded, "You really heard me." This was the day

I knew we had learned how to communicate. You can read more about these insights in **Speaking the Truth in Love** in which I share what I have learned about communicating.

I was able to hear her and be completely present because I was believing the gospel, was rooted and grounded in Christ, and was not taking what she said defensively or personally. In the past, whenever Sandi would request time to talk, internally I would go on the defensive. Outwardly I would be cool and in control, but inside I would be scrambling to figure out what the topic was, where I had messed up, and already had calls in to the defense attorney part of my brain. Then when we sat down, only 25 percent of my brain would be fully engaged in listening, as most of my team was planning my response and how to defend what was being said. I was not putting myself in her shoes. I was not being empathetic about her needs; I was dealing with my own stuff while in damage control mode. I may be overstating this, but not by much.

Knowing God likes me just as I am, that He gets me, accepts me, and is working in my heart, sets me free to be vulnerable and transparent. I am able to let God take care of me and thus am able to enter her world and hear her pain and what she is feeling. I have also learned communication skills and how to ask questions to draw out more information so I can understand what she is saying as much as possible. But even with the skills and tools we have at our disposal now, knowing God has my back and is for me, frees me up to love her from my heart. When my heart is right, then the tongue follows.

I am also learning my focus is to work with God in this business of personal transformation. My job description is only concerned with me, not anyone else. God is the only one qualified to fix people. I can't fix anyone, particularly my wife or children. It is a full-time job just focusing on myself. My responsibility for others is to love them as God has loved me.

I have learned an important lesson which applies to the body of Christ. God does the fixing, the church does the loving. We are called to bear each other's burdens, pray for each other, build each other up, and encourage one another. Knowing we are all messy, all changing, all with baggage and wounds from the past, helps me love and accept others, because this is how God loves and accepts me. We may cover up our unsightly messes, but God sees them and still loves us.

As a parent, I know I have the potential to impact the lives of my children. When I obey God, they are positively affected, and when I sin, there are repercussions to the "the third and fourth generation of those who hate me, but showing steadfast love to thousands of those who love me and keep my commandments." (Deuteronomy 5:9-10) I have always known this truth, but what I have learned in the past few years is my stuff, my own issues, will also have an effect on those closest to me. It will come out and it won't be pretty. I need to face it, bring it to the light, get help, either from friends and/or professional therapists.

But this is hard work and painful. I could not have faced, accepted, or embraced my stuff without knowing God loves, likes, knows, and accepts me for who I am. Having the assurance God is on my team, that He has my back and faces my painful past with me, has made all the difference. With the conviction God likes me, I am also learning to like and accept myself and be comfortable in my own skin. With God's help, I have been able to do a good bit of dying, which has led to new life, as Jesus predicted. Being the grain of wheat which has fallen into the earth and died, has borne good fruit in my relationships with my wife and sons.

Not only did this crisis bring me to Christ in a new way, along the way I met the Holy Spirit and am developing a special connection with Him. I grew in my understanding of my heavenly Dad. I love Him and look forward with joy to spending time communicating and being with Him. I have discovered some of the benefits of pain, am communicating better with my wife, comprehending the power of the gospel in a deeper way, and am daily appreciating grace. I am in the best place with my wife and family and have found a cadre of true friends who have faithfully borne my burdens with me. I am a rich man.

I also see my own baggage inhibited my ability to see God for who is truly is, merciful, gracious, slow to anger, and full of lovingkindness and truth. He is not distant, impossible to please, and generally disappointed with me. He is my Dad. He loves me all the time in every way, and lights up when I draw near to Him, every time.

Hope for Fallen Saints

I have a very perceptive sister in the Lord with whom I had many deep conversations in 2012. In one of our talks we discussed those saints who should have know better and still sinned. The church seems harsh towards these fallen brothers and sisters. As believers, we seem to have no trouble forgiving Paul for his sins, because they were committed before he met Jesus on the road to Damascus. But what about Peter, who had spent years with Jesus and then betrayed Him. Or David, who knew God, and yet committed adultery and murder?

She writes, "Ah, that resonates. And I believe it is true. There are places for the 'Pauls' to receive grace, but fewer for the 'Peters, Davids, etc'. It is acceptable to vent your horrible struggles and sins on one side of the cross, because after all, even Paul killed Christians before Damascus. But we're not so keen on hearing from or hanging with Peter or the others because they should have known better, having walked with God as they did. We frankly see their conduct as inexcusable. So, even if God forgives them, we don't, particularly if we have the notion that we are responsible for setting them up in a position of leadership or authority. Instead, it is just easier to make the pretty church uninhabitable for exposed Christians. So these expatriates wander around lost, having fallen short of the glory of man.

The ministry community, whether pastoral, home schooling, or just being a leader, does not seem to to have any hospitals to retreat to if you fall ill. There are plenty of places to work--plenty of places to serve, and showcase, and certainly a penal system, but not many benches, parks, therapists, or (honestly), confessionals."

Another friend who fell into sin as a Christian, did not know where to go for help. Throughout her church experience she heard many testimonies of people who lived sordid lives before coming to faith, and then were freed and forgiven by Christ when they were born again. But she never heard a testimony of someone who had faithfully Jesus followed for years, and then sinned, share the details of how they were convicted, forgiven, and subsequently restored to fellowship.

Thank God we have the accounts of David and Peter being restored to full fellowship and even positions of leadership. May God help us to embrace of Redeemer God of grace who is more than able to make ALL THINGS work together for good.

Loose Ends

Since I have shared my story about my crisis at conferences and other speaking events, I have heard from many others who are going through similar trials. While I have received emails and phone calls from a few men, it is usually a desperate wife who will reach out and wonder what they should do. The situation at home is becoming unbearable and the wife and children are desperate. Our story, for it includes all members of our family, has given them hope, that perhaps they can be restored and reconciled as well.

As I mentioned in Chapter 2, I have heard many stories that did not turn out like our story. The husband may acknowledge his faults and pursue counseling but his wife does not. Or the wife will read books and seek help, but the husband is not willing. As I have reflected on why we were able to make it, I think it was because all of us were committed to the process. Sandi, Isaac, Ethan, Joseph, and John, were on board with being healed and staying together as a family. God helped us.

But what if Sandi had sought help and support from the Christian community, and was walking in integrity, and I did not respond. What if she, upon receiving counsel, had drawn a line in the sand, and I was unwilling to get help or to change? The story would not have had a happy ending in our eyes and I would probably not have written this book. Sadly, she eventually would have had to leave for the pain would have been unendurable. What then?

I find comfort in the end of the faith chapter in Hebrews 11. After recounting all the extraordinary exploits of people of faith from Abel to Moses the author continues by writing: "How much more do I need to say? It would take too long to recount the stories of the faith of Gideon, Barak, Samson,

Jephthah, David, Samuel, and all the prophets. By faith these people overthrew kingdoms, ruled with justice, and received what God had promised them. They shut the mouths of lions, quenched the flames of fire, and escaped death by the edge of the sword. Their weakness was turned to strength. They became strong in battle and put whole armies to flight. Women received their loved ones back again from death." (Hebrews 11:32-35 NLT)

And then he paints another picture beginning with the ominous word "But." "But others were tortured, refusing to turn from God in order to be set free. They placed their hope in a better life after the resurrection. Some were jeered at, and their backs were cut open with whips. Others were chained in prisons. Some died by stoning, some were sawed in half, and others were killed with the sword. Some went about wearing skins of sheep and goats, destitute and oppressed and mistreated. They were too good for this world, wandering over deserts and mountains, hiding in caves and holes in the ground. All these people earned a good reputation because of their faith, yet none of them received all that God had promised." (Hebrews 11:35-39 NLT)

These people also had faith, but they did not have the same results as their brethren. There is no formula to guarantee a particular outcome. God is the author and finisher of our faith. He is the Redeemer. He will work ALL things together for our good. It is our responsibility to cleave to Him, commit our way to Him, and trust Him for the results.

Prayer

"May our Lord Jesus Christ himself, and God our Father who loved us and gave us eternal comfort and good hope through grace, comfort your hearts and establish them in every good work and word." (2 Thessalonians 2:16–17)

QUESTIONS FOR REFLECTION

1. What does change require, according to Steve's experience?

2. Think about the "cracked pot" image. What does it mean to you? How does it help you forgive yourself?

3. *"...let the world, the flesh, and the devil be your only enemies and don't help them by beating yourself up. This is the job of our enemy, the accuser of the brethren."* Jot your response to this quote. Do you agree with it? Why or why not?

4. In the business of personal transformation, what is your job description?

5. What important lesson which applies to the body of Christ has Steve learned?

CONCLUSION

If you have read thus far, you know when I refer to my stuff, I am including past wounds, hurts, and baggage. As I reflect, I see more clearly the impact my stuff had on the two most vital of commands from God, to love God with everything in me, and to love others as I have been loved.

When God first revealed the good news of His love for me on a ranch in Colorado, my heart was awakened and I was born from above. I became a new creature. In 2012, God revealed more of His love for me and I began to comprehend in a deeper way how much He loved and liked me for who I was and not based on what I do. As I apprehended His unconditional divine affection for me, I found myself loving Him more, which is the first and great commandment according to Jesus.

Meditating on how God has loved me, has equipped me to love my wife and children in similar unconditional ways, which is the new commandment.

With God's help, I am enjoying a deeper and more meaningful relationship with the Trinity, learning to love others as I have been loved, and minimizing pain to those who are closest to me. For this I am eternally grateful.

God has encouraged me to put pen to paper and write this book. He made me know I was to be faithful to what I had lived through and not wait until I was a "writer." In other words, I am enough right now. I hope these words have been an encouragement to you. Thank you for reading.

Note: I am revising this book in 2018 and I confess it is not enjoyable to read. God and my family have continued to extend grace to me, and while I am in a good place with my Dad and my family, my joy is still mingled with a trace of sorrow. But I am okay with this. I ponder how David continued after seeing the havoc his sin created in his home. But with God's help, he was able to fully own His sin (Psalm 51) and continue to worship and serve the God he loved. May we each do likewise.

Prayer

"Since then we have a great high priest who has passed through the heavens, Jesus, the Son of God, let us hold fast our confession. For we do not have a high priest who is unable to sympathize with our weaknesses, but one who in every respect has been tempted as we are, yet without sin. Let us then with confidence draw near to the throne of grace, that we may receive mercy and find grace to help in time of need." (Hebrews 4:14)

ABOUT THE AUTHOR

Steve Demme and his wife Sandra have been married since 1979. They have been blessed with four sons, three lovely daughters-in-law, and three special grandchildren.

Steve has served in full or part time pastoral ministry for many years after graduating from Gordon-Conwell Theological Seminary. He is the creator of Math-U-See and the founder of Building Faith Families and has served on the board of Joni and Friends, PA.

He produces a monthly newsletter, weekly podcasts, and regular posts https://www.facebook.com/stevedemme/

Steve is a regular speaker at home education conferences, men's ministry events, and family retreats. His desire is to strengthen, teach, encourage, validate, and exhort parents and families to follow the biblical model for the Christian home.

BUILDING FAITH FAMILIES

Exists to teach and encourage families to embrace the biblical model for the Christian home.

Scripture declares God created the sacred institution of the family. In His wisdom, He designed marriage to be between one man and one woman. We believe healthy God-fearing families are the basic building block for the church and society.

The family is foundational and transformational. Parents and children become more like Jesus as they lay their lives down for each other, pray for each other, and learn to love each other as God has loved them.

RESOURCES TO ENCOURAGE AND STRENGTHEN YOUR FAMILY

- The **Monthly Newsletter** is an encouraging exhortation as well as updates on Bible contests and upcoming speaking engagements.

- Podcast Each week an episode is released on our website, Itunes, and our Facebook page. These may be downloaded for free.

- **Seminars for free download** For over 20 years Steve has been speaking and teaching at conferences around the world. Many of his messages are available for your edification.

- **Like us on Facebook** for updates of new podcasts, speaking engagements, and new resources for your home and family.

www.buildingfaithfamilies.org

KNOWING GOD'S LOVE,

BECOMING ROOTED AND GROUNDED IN GRACE

Comprehending God's unconditional love is the cornerstone for the overarching commands to love God and our neighbor. For we are unable to love until we have first been loved. "We love, because He first loved us." (1 John 4:19) and "In this is love, not that we have loved God but that he loved us." (1 John 4:10)

The first, or as Jesus called it, the Great Command, is to love God. I began asking God to help me love Him with all my heart, soul, mind, and strength and was wonderfully surprised by how he answered my request.

Instead of awaking one morning with a burning love for God, which I expected, He began to steadily reveal how much He loved me. In 2012 I found myself believing in a new way that God knows me thoroughly and loves me completely. This knowledge that God likes me for who I am, and not based on what I do, has transformed my life.

As I have become more rooted and grounded in grace, my relationship with God is now much richer and deeper. My wife and I are closer than we have ever been. Knowing I am loved and accepted just as I am, has freed me to be more transparent and real as I relate with my sons and others.

TRANSFORMED IN LOVE,

LOVING OTHERS AS JESUS HAS LOVED US

John 15:9 revealed God not only loved the world, He loved me. Jesus says to His disciples, "As the Father has loved me, so have I loved you. Abide in my love." Just as the Father loved His Son, Jesus loves me the same way.

The secret to abiding in God's love is found in the next few verses. "If you keep my commandments, you will abide in my love, just as I have kept my Father's commandments and abide in His love. This is my commandment, that you love one another as I have loved you." (John 15:10, 12)

As I love others, as I have been loved, I will abide in the love of God. As a husband and father, my primary responsibilities are to love God, my wife, and my sons. I am writing as a man and sharing how God has led me to begin applying these principles in our home. But these principles are applicable to every believer.

The fruit of loving others as we have been loved will not only bless each of our homes, but our communities as well. "By this all people will know that you are my disciples, if you have love for one another." (John 13:34)

As family members pray for one another, bear each other's burdens, lay their lives down for each other, and learn to love one another as Jesus has loved them, they are transformed and become more like Jesus.

SPEAKING THE TRUTH IN LOVE,

LESSONS I'VE LEARNED ABOUT
FAMILY COMMUNICATION

Most of what I've learned about communication, I acquired in the past few years during transitioning my business to a family owned business. The ability to communicate about difficult topics like business, values, your occupation, and a family's legacy takes effort and training.

As a husband and father, I have the potential to build up and encourage my family like no one else. I also have the ability to tear down and discourage my wife and sons. The Bible teaches effective principles of communication which are timeless.

My relationship with my wife and children has been transformed through godly safe communication. As I continue to grow in grace and the knowledge of God, I am in a better place to have open, transparent, and honest communication. While the skills we have acquired in being a clear speaker and an engaged listener are beneficial, investing time to have a quiet heart is essential. For out of the abundance of the heart, the mouth speaks.

I hope the principles we have learned and applied to such benefit in our own home and business will be a help to you on your journey. May the words of our mouth and the meditation of our heart be acceptable in your sight, O LORD, our Rock and our Redeemer. (from Psalms 19:14)

THE CHRISTIAN HOME
AND FAMILY WORSHIP

In this readable and encouraging book, Steve shares practical scripture-based tips for teaching the word of God to children of all ages.

He also addresses common obstacles we all face in establishing the discipline of regular family worship.

Be encouraged by Steve's experiences teaching his four sons, and learn from other families who share strategies that have worked for their children. You may purchase this book, or participate in our Family Worship Challenge.

When you read or listen to *"The Christian Home and Family Worship"* within 30 days of receiving your copy, it is yours for FREE. If you are unable to fulfill this obligation, you agree to send a check for $50.00 to Building Faith Families. Steve will follow up with you at the end of thirty days. Contact Steve at sdemme@demmelearning.com

"I loved the book and read it in about a week and a half. My chief take-away was family worship needs to be an important part of family life. I've had five family worship times and I can definitely say I've already seen some fruits from these sessions. Your book had some great examples of how to make it more appealing to the kids."

"I was indeed able to read the book in time. The main thing I took away from it was the Nike slogan: "Just do it." So I did.

STEWARDSHIP

"Where your treasure is, there will your heart be also." (Luke 12:34)

There are two components addressed in Stewardship, our treasure and our heart. God calls us to love Him with all our heart and be faithful stewards of our God-given treasure. Half of the curriculum is focused on our relationship with God and the other half with being wise stewards of our treasure. It is appropriate for anyone with a good grasp of basic math and who has completed Algebra 1.

Stewardship Instruction Pack
The Stewardship Instruction Pack contains the instruction manual with lesson-by-lesson instructions, detailed solutions, and the DVD with lesson-by-lesson video instruction.

Discipleship Material
Steve references hundreds of scriptures from Genesis to Revelation in sharing how God has helped him to apply biblical principles in his home, business, and personal walk with God. He also shares a plethora of topical studies on essential components of discipleship. Students are encouraged to read the complete New Testament during the course as well.

STEWARDSHIP

Stewardship Student Pack

The Stewardship Student Pack contains the Student Workbook with lesson-by-lesson worksheets, and review pages. It also includes the Stewardship Tests.

A Sampling of "Treasure Topics"
- Earning Money
- Taxes
- Banking and Interest
- Credit Cards
- Comparison Shopping
- Costs for Operating an Automobile
- Wise Charitable Giving
- Starting Your Own Business, and more

A Taste of "Heart Studies"
- The Love of Money
- Trusting God and Being Content
- Purchase with Prayer
- Work is a God Thing
- Our Identity in Christ
- The Inspired Word of God
- Honor Your Father and Mother
- Guard Your Heart

Thanks for this curriculum! This was the best math course I've taken in all my high school years, and I don't even like math :)

- Caleb

That your curriculum is Christ-centered has made the biggest difference in my homeschool experience.

- Sarah

THE HYMNS FOR FAMILY WORSHIP

This time-honored collection of 100 classic hymns will be a rich addition to your family worship. Make a joyful noise to the LORD!

In addition to the music for these carefully selected songs of worship, the history and origin of each hymn enhances the meaning of the lyrics.

There are four CDs with piano accompaniment for singing along in your home, car, or church.

Some of the titles are:

- What a Friend We Have in Jesus
- Holy, Holy, Holy
- It Is Well With My Soul
- To God Be The Glory
- All Hail the Power of Jesus Name
- Amazing Grace
- How Firm a Foundation
- Blessed Assurance
- Christ Arose
- Rise Up O Men of God
- Jesus Paid It All
- Just As I Am, along with 88 more!

Made in the USA
Columbia, SC
17 June 2018